TÀIJÍ JIÀN

32-Posture Sword Form

of related interest

Tàijíquán
Li Deyin
Foreword by Siu-Fong Evans
ISBN 978 1 84819 004 7

Eternal Spring
Taiji Quan, Qi Gong and the Cultivation of Health, Happiness and Longevity
Michael Acton
ISBN 978 1 84819 003 0

Tai Chi Chuan and the Code of Life
Revealing the Deeper Mysteries of China's Ancient Art for Health and Harmony
– Revised Edition
Graham Horwood
ISBN 978 1 84819 001 6

Bagua Daoyin
A Unique Branch of Daoist Learning – A Secret Skill of the Palace
He Jinghan
Translated by David Alexander
ISBN 978 1 84819 009 2

TÀIJÍ JIÀN

32-POSTURE SWORD FORM

James Drewe

SINGING DRAGON
London and Philadelphia

First published in 2009 by
Singing Dragon
An imprint of Jessica Kingsley Publishers
116 Pentonville Road
London N1 9JB, UK

www.jkp.com

The photographs in this book feature Simon Watson of the Longfei Taijiquan Association.
All photographs were taken by Simon Butcher of Zebu Design.

Library of Congress Cataloging in Publication Data
Drewe, James.
Taiji jian 32-posture sword form / James Drewe.
p. cm.
ISBN 978-1-84819-011-5 (pb : alk. paper) 1. Tai chi. 2. Swordplay. I. Title. II. Title: Taiji
jian thirty-two-posture sword form.
GV504.D74 2009
796.815'5--dc22
2008022623

British Library Cataloguing in Publication Data
A CIP catalogue record for this book is available from the British Library
Printed and bound by CPI Group (UK) Ltd, Croydon, CR0 4YY

ISBN 978 1 84819 011 5

Contents

Chapter 1: Introduction

Note on Pronunciation of Chinese Words 7

Chinese Weapons 8

The Jiàn 8

A Brief History of the Jiàn 9

Blade Construction 10

Parts of the Jiàn 11

The Balance of the Sword 15

Holding the Sword 15

Performing Taiji and Taiji Sword 17

Two-Person Sword Routines 18

Traditional and Modern 18

The Sword Metaphysically 19

Intention 20

Development of the 32-Posture Sword Form 21

The 13 Applications 22

Chapter 2: Techniques

Sword Strokes 23

Stances 34

Footwork 40

The Sword-Fingers 41

Definitions of Terms Used 45

Chapter 3: The Form

Opening the Form 49

Section 1 61

Section 2 92

Section 3 122

Section 4 154

Closing the Form 186

Chapter 4: Summary

Footprint Map of the Form 190

Summary of the Form 207

Chapter 5: Beyond the Basics

The 32-Posture Sword Form in Competition 216

Music for the 32-Posture Sword Form 217

Centre-Movement 1 217

ABOUT THE AUTHOR 221

FURTHER READING 223

CHAPTER **1**

Introduction

This book is based upon information obtained from several teachers, and a very limited number of books, most of which are in Chinese. The 32-Posture Sword Form, from the point of view of the physical movements only, is not complex, but there is a significant amount of other information, relating to the applications, that is open to interpretation. Although there are 13 textbook applications, some of which are repeated several times, there are others that occur during the movements that lead up to the position by which the final Posture is known.

I have been wary about over-emphasizing these other applications because they are not considered as important as the main 13 – in fact it would seem that they are considered to be definitely *un*important, presumably because the structure of the Form is such that each of the 32 Postures is completed by an application – although there are a couple of exceptions. Therefore, if you started to include all the other applications, you would have more than a *32-Posture* Sword Form. However, I have mentioned them in such a way that they are separated from the main text, and they should be looked upon as interesting possibilities or interpretations, rather than textbook fact.

With the very generous help of John Fairbairn, I have tried to ensure that the translations of the Chinese names and terms are as accurate as possible, but as always with translations from the Chinese, there is some flexibility in the meaning of the words. Therefore, some of these should not be read too critically.

I would like to thank Professor Li Deyin, Master Wang Yan Ji, Hui Yip, and Simon Watson, for all their help and patience in answering many persistent questions, and in particular Richard Watson for all his help and for the many lengthy discussions that we have had on the subject over many years. I think that all of us are keen to have a reliable textbook in English on the subject, and I have therefore been at pains to be as detailed, and as accurate, as possible.

Note on Pronunciation of Chinese Words

The Chinese language uses four 'tones', or inflections of the voice, and one 'neutral' tone, and these have been rendered in the text as closely as possible.

Tone 1	(a flat tone)	:	āēīōū
Tone 2	(a rising tone)	:	áéíóú
Tone 3	(a falling/rising tone)	:	ǎěǐǒǔ
Tone 4	(a falling tone)	:	àèìòù
Tone 5	(a neutral tone)	:	aeiou

Therefore, a word such as 行步 **xing2bu4** will be written as **xíngbù**.

Chinese Weapons

Chinese weapons are usually classified into three categories, two of which are dependent upon range, and a third that fits into neither of these categories.

Long-range weapons are those such as the long staff (cháng máo 长矛; gùn 棍), the spear (qiāng 枪), and the halberd (máo 矛).

Short-range weapons are those such as the double-edged sword (jiàn 剑), the sabre or broadsword (dāndāo 单刀), and various knives/daggers.

Other weapons are the fan (shàn 扇), the whip, the three-section staff, and hidden weapons such as needles and darts.

Of all these weapons, the one that is closest to the jiàn is the sabre, and for this reason alone it is worth mentioning it briefly.

It differs from the jiàn in that the blade is curved like a cutlass, scimitar, saif (Arabic), Shamshir (Persian), and Kilij (Turkish). This is a single-edged blade (a backsword), the unsharpened edge of which usually curves upwards slightly. In English this weapon is usually referred to as a 'broadsword' because of the shape of the blade which, from the hilt, starts narrowly, but gradually broadens before rapidly narrowing again at the tip. Having said that, there are some Chinese versions that do not broaden in the manner described above, and which closer resemble the 19th century British cavalry officer's weapon. This weapon is mainly for hacking and chopping!

The Jiàn

The jiàn is a straight double-edged sword which weighs anywhere from about 2–3¾ pounds. The total length of the weapon is approximately 3 feet; the length of the blade varies as it is dependent upon the height of the person who uses it. The traditional method of determining the appropriate length is by holding the handle of the sword so that the blade is vertical and against the back of your straightened arm; the tip should be at the same level as the ear lobe (although some practitioners like it to reach the top of the ear).

The other method of measuring the correct length to suit the individual is that the length of the entire sword – pommel to tip – should be the same as the distance from the user's navel to the ground.

The double-edged blade is 1½–2 inches wide.

Nowadays there are many types of double-edged Tàijí swords that can be bought, but many of the more springy Wushu blades, or blades with no 'give' at all, are best avoided. There needs to be a slight spring, but not so much that the blade would not support itself if the tip were rested on the ground. Some of the modern blades are so flexible that the tips can bend in a full circle, and still spring back to their original position. These can give a thoroughly satisfying fā-jìn[1] 'wobble' and even produce a sound, but unfortunately, they are no measure of any kind of skill as a child can also produce the same result. On the other hand, a blade that is too solid is unable to produce any kind of Fa-Jing effect at all.

A heavy sword may be tiring to use, although this does also depend upon the balance of the weapon. Conversely, one that is too light will not feel as though it is a part of your body, and will not *carry itself* through the movements; it will more than likely be quite unsatisfying to use.

A Brief History of the Jiàn

The earliest known Chinese double-edged swords were produced during the time of Huang Di, the 'Yellow Emperor' (2697–2597 B.C.), and initially,

---

1   Fā jìn (发劲 explosive energy/force) is the production of sudden power from the body. It is more than a muscular punch; it is the involvement of the entire body in an action, but in a split second.

these were mostly copper swords. By the Shang Dynasty (1766–1122 B.C.), swords were being made of bronze, an alloy of copper and tin; by about 1200 B.C., iron swords were introduced. During the Spring and Autumn Period (722–475 B.C. – though there appears to be some disagreement on these dates), the skill of sword smiths and the quality of the swords reached the highest level yet. These earlier swords were shorter, wider, and thicker, but the Qin Dynasty (221–206 B.C.) saw the perfection of the bronze sword, and the swords became longer, narrower, and thinner. By the Tang Dynasty (A.D. 618–907), one of the more peaceful periods of Chinese history, the double-edged sword had developed to the shape that we know today, and was being made from steel.

Nowadays, there are many types of jiàn, and the main difference is usually in the hilt, in particular in the design, decoration, and/or weight of the guard and pommel. These swords are available almost anywhere today, and are made not only in China but also in the USA, and the UK; they are easily purchased through the Internet and are often of a very high quality.

Blade Construction

Two of the most important features when producing a sword are to make the edge as hard as possible, so that it will cope with wear and tear, and to make the length of the blade resilient, so that it is able to stand up to hard treatment.

As hard steel can shatter, and resilient steel implies a softness which is less able to keep an edge, these two objectives seem to be rather contradictory.

However, the Chinese smiths achieved this by combining both hard and soft steels in a variety of ways:

1. Harder steel was wrapped around a softer core of steel.

2. A thin blade of harder steel was produced, and this was sandwiched between softer steel 'cups' for the length of the blade, thereby widening the 'faces', 'flats', 'ridges', or sides of the blade.

3. Both harder and softer layers of steel were twisted and then hammered together.

In all cases, the blade, or part of the blade, would then be treated by a method called 'differential hardening' which increased the hardness of the edge without causing the whole blade to become brittle. By this method, the edge of the blade only is 'quenched' (rapidly cooled), whilst the central spine of the blade is insulated with (for example) clay; or it can also be achieved without the insulation by pouring water only on to the edge of the blade.

Parts of the Jiàn

There are four basic parts:

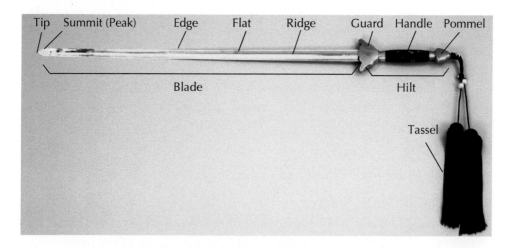

Tip Summit (Peak) Edge Flat Ridge Guard Handle Pommel

Blade   Hilt

Tassel

1. Blade – (劍身 jiàn shēn or 劍体 jiàn tǐ)

This is the overall name for the length of steel that forms the sword, usually about 26–36 inches in length.

The Chinese divide this into three sections:

- The first third of the blade (although some would argue the first 6–8 inches), including the tip, is called the qián rèn (前刃 the front edge). It is comparatively thin and flexible, and is razor sharp. It is easily broken, and it is used not for blocking, but for attacking.

- The middle third of the blade is called the zhōng rèn (中刃 the middle edge) and is thicker, and less sharp. It is used for diverting (intercepting), and cutting or chopping.

- The final third of the blade nearest the hilt is called the jiàn gēn (劍根 the jiàn root) and is blunt and unsharpened. It is used for blocking an opponent's blade, or pushing him away.

(In the West, the blade is divided into two parts: the **foible** – the part of the blade between the middle and the tip, and the **forte** – the part of the blade between the hilt and the middle.)

A jiàn blade has seven areas (see diagram):

Edge – (劍刃 jiàn rèn).
The sharpest and thinnest part of the blade. The edge is further separated into the **upper edge** and the **lower edge.**

Tip – (劍尖 jiàn jiān).
The end of the sword furthest away from the hilt; the extreme sharpened point. Most Chinese swords taper to a point at the tip, but some of the earlier ones had parallel edges until about 1 inch from the end when it would abruptly taper to a tip.

Flat – (劍面 jiàn miàn).
The side of the blade. This is also called the **face** of the blade.

Back/Spine/(Median) Ridge – (劍脊 jiàn jǐ).
The middle and relatively convex part of the sword which runs almost the full length of the blade, although it will flatten out towards the tip.

Fuller – Often called the blood groove or gutter, the fuller is a narrow groove that runs most of the length of many swords. The general view is that it is there to allow the blade to be easily removed by blood escaping through the channel, thereby reducing suction as the wound tries to close. Contrary to popular belief, this is not the case, although it may be a by-product. The actual reason for the fuller is to lighten the blade whilst actually strengthening it, in the same way that a steel 'I' beam is stronger than a solid piece of steel. Use of a fuller allows a sword smith to use less material to comprise the blade, making it lighter without sacrificing too much structural integrity.

Ricasso – Found on some swords, the ricasso is the unsharpened part of the blade just before the guard. Strictly speaking, it is the flattened area between the end of the medial ridge and the guard.

It was typically used on heavier swords to provide a place to grip with the second hand if needed. The ricasso is a later feature, appearing from the late Qing Dynasty onward, and reflects European influence.

Tang – The portion of the blade that is covered by the hilt. A full tang is the same width as the rest of the blade and extends beyond the hilt and through

12

the pommel. A partial tang does not extend all the way through the hilt and is normally not more than half the width of the blade. The length of the tang and the width, particularly where it narrows before entering the pommel, vary from sword to sword. The thickness and width of a tang within the hilt will determine the handling of the sword.

The end of the tang may be threaded, with a **nut** securing the blade to the grip.

There is one other identifiable part of the blade that is mentioned in some Tàijí sword books. This is the **peak** or **summit** of the blade, where the angle of the edge of the blade alters from a straight line, and falls towards the tip – usually approximately 1 inch from the tip (劍峰 jiàn fēng).

(For the sake of completeness, the '**back**' is the part of the blade opposite the edge. A double-edged sword (i.e. the jiàn) has no back, whereas a sabre or broadsword has one.)

2. Hilt – (劍把 jiàn bà)

The hilt often refers to the **fittings**, as well as to the actual handle or grip. The jiàn hilt fittings – in order of attachment – consist of the **hand guard**, a **ferrule** (wide metal ring approximately 1 inch wide) between the hand guard and the actual **handle** or **grip**, another ferrule after the handle, and then the end piece or **pommel**. Jiàn fittings are generally of brass or bronze, and less frequently of German silver.

The Fittings
A general name for the hand guard, the parts of the handle (ferrules and grip), and the pommel.

Often these would be very ornate, studded with gems, possibly engraved, or with gilt bronze or silver decorations, pierced brass, or set with carved jade.

Hand Guard – (劍格 jiàn gé or 护手 hù shou).
The metal piece that prevents an opponent's sword from reaching your hand.

Handle/Grip – (劍柄 jiàn bǐng or 劍把 jiàn bà or the 'old term' is 劍莖 jiàn jīng).
The part of the hilt that is gripped by the hand.

It is usually made of wood, and is fastened to the **tang** of the blade to provide a comfortable way of holding the sword. Often the handle is covered with stingray skin, as it provides an excellent non-slip surface, and the skin is sometimes stained green. Other handles might be of plain or carved wood or horn, and may be of varying lengths.

Pommel – (劍首 jiàn shǒu).
The end of the sword to which the hilt is attached.

Pommels are normally wider than the circumference of the hilt and keep the sword from sliding out of the hand, as well as providing a bit of counterweight to the blade. They also can be used as a means to secure the hilt to the tang, and were usually forged out of the same piece of steel as the rest of the blade.

3. Tassel – (劍穗 **jiàn suì** or 劍袍 **jiàn páo**)

It is questionable as to the martial use of the tassel; however, there are several suggestions for its addition:

1. The tassel came in two alternative lengths – one was the length of the sword; the other was the length of half of the sword. This tassel was of a strong rope, presumably fine, and enabled the user to throw the sword like a spear at an opponent, whilst he held on to the end of the tassel.

2. The tassel could be used against the eyes of an opponent, or to distract him – strands of metal might have been intertwined in the ropes.

3. To improve the balance of the sword.

4. For show, demonstration, and for use in dance – to improve the aesthetic look.

5. To be wound around the wrist during combat to lessen the chance of losing the weapon.

I would have thought that (1) was unlikely, as more likely than not it would be a hindrance, and an opponent could easily catch it, or cut it if the sword were thrown. (2) is possible, although, as above, the chance of becoming entangled with it oneself would seem highly likely. (3) also seems unlikely, as the obvious way of improving the balance of a sword is to make alterations to the fittings of the weapon, and (4) and (5) would appear to be by far the most likely.

4. Scabbard (劍鞘 jiàn qiào)

The sheath of the sword was usually wooden, but sometimes made of metal (which could also be used as a blocking weapon). It might be surfaced with dyed shagreen (untanned leather with a roughened surface, usually dyed green), or covered in stingray skin (which was then lacquered or stained), or simply decorated with a coloured lacquer. Stingray skin, whilst still being light, adds considerable strength to the scabbard.

The scabbard supported various metal fittings, usually of brass or bronze: A **throat piece** (where the sword enters the scabbard), two or three **suspension bands** (for attaching the scabbard to the belt), and a metal cap (or tip cover) called a **chape** at the scabbard-point.

Some scabbards would cause the sword to be ejected from the scabbard when a clip was released.

The Balance of the Sword

Since old swords were made with the function of combat foremost in mind, they were generally very well balanced. A well-balanced blade is not only far less tiring to handle, and therefore far more energy-efficient, but it also enables the user to handle a heavier weapon that might otherwise have been impossible with a badly balanced blade. In Tàijí terms, this means that it is easier to feel 'the sword doing the work' for you, rather than your making an extra effort to *wield* the sword. It therefore encourages Tàijí principles.

The balance point of a jiàn should be no more than 4 inches up the blade from the point where the blade enters the hand guard.

There are several ways to improve the balance of a jiàn, including adding weight to the pommel, replacing the pommel with a heavier one, lengthening the handle, or a combination of these methods.

Holding the Sword

The 'V' of the thumb and index finger should be aligned with one of the raised edges of the guard; the 'web' of skin should be close to the guard. This is similar in concept to the left hand position of a right-handed golfer (see picture a).

15

The sword should be held lightly, and quite loosely, with often only the thumb, index, and middle fingers supporting the weapon. The ring and little fingers tend to act as controllers, particularly when using a flat blade (i.e. the sides/faces or flats of the blade facing sky and floor) (see pictures b and c).

There should be flexibility in the fingers and wrist, which will thereby allow the wrist freer movement in all directions, and it is therefore important to avoid holding the sword with an iron grip, as this causes the wrist to freeze up (see pictures d, e and f).

Hold the sword in the same way that you might hold a table-tennis bat; you only tighten your grip when you need to (see picture g).

16

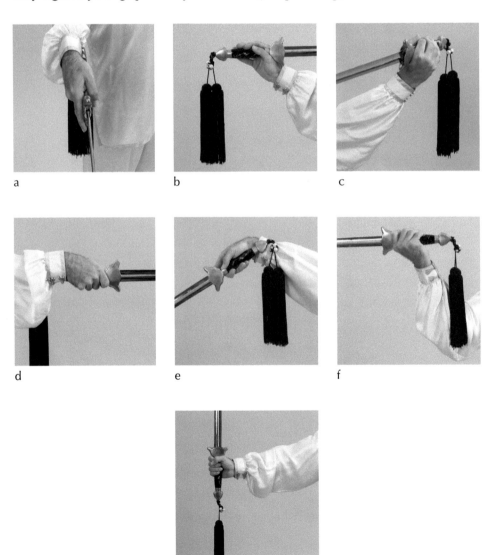

a   b   c

d   e   f

g

Performing Tàijí and Tàijí Sword

- All movements should be performed in as relaxed a manner as possible. There should be no breaks between the movements, which should be even and soft. This does *not* mean that the speed of the various movements is absolutely constant. It is quite usual and desirable to slow the movement down as you move into a posture – although this shouldn't be overdone! It is the equivalent of 'rubato' (lit. 'robbed time') in music, and is the difference between *doing* the moves and *interpreting* the moves; it is the *feel* of the movements.

- The entire body should be relaxed, but the body should be *lengthened*, as though reaching its full natural height. This does not mean that you stretch upwards, rather that you give your body a direction in which to relax – in this case upwards from feet to crown (and across the body also, from hand to hand). The Tàijí expression is to 'raise the crown as though suspended by a silken thread'. The principle is the same as a healthy plant growing; it grows upwards towards the sky, as the roots grow downwards. Avoid performing Tàijí as though you are wilting!

- Ensure that your breathing is smooth, slow, even, and calm.

- Every movement is initiated by the foot, controlled by the waist, transmitted to the wrist, and manifested in the blade or tip of the sword. Therefore, there should be good upper body and lower body coordination; even the slightest transference of weight from one foot to another should be reflected throughout the body.

- Further to the above, many students perform Tàijí (both Hand and Sword Forms) as though their arms have an independent intelligence. It is essential that the core of the body moves the sword. If the body is still, the sword will not move. This gives immense power to the sword, and in fact, it is then moved by internal power (qì 气). The sword should feel as though it is an extension of your body.

- Ensure that your body is stable at every point of a movement. When placing a foot, for example, place it so that it can be retracted if necessary, and only then do you commit your weight on to it. You should be able to stop at a moment's notice in the middle of any movement and feel that you are stable. This will allow you to become light and nimble if necessary, and will give you speed should you need it.

- Every movement should be directed by your intention (yì 意). Your mind is extended to whichever part of the sword you are using. This means that it is important to understand the applications of each posture, otherwise it is hard to know what the intention is! Understanding the application of a move allows the movements to become more accurate; this does not mean that you move faster when performing a move or posture, nor is the speed of the Form jerky and uneven.

Two-Person Sword Routines

There are a number of two-person Forms (movement-sets) and drills, particularly modern ones.

The two-person Forms, e.g. the Sun style, Wudang style, or 'Yuan Yang' sword ('two of a kind' or 'a pair') two-person routines, are Forms that interact, so that one person is usually attacking, and the other defending, and vice versa. More often than not, the defence will be to avoid the strike (perhaps by side-stepping), and then to 'defend by striking'. They are difficult to learn and, to be understood completely, require both halves of the Form to be learnt, as both sides differ. They are the equivalent of the San Shou two-person hand routines.

The two-person drills are not unlike Pushing Hands, with which most Tàijí practitioners will be familiar.

As in Pushing Hands, the principles of adhering and following apply, and some of the drills use similar small circular movements – one person thrusting as the other parries, and then the other way around.

Other drills use the principle of evade-and-attack-from-safety; therefore, good footwork and balance are a priority.

The drills generally avoid blocking with the blade, even on the blunt end near the hilt, and blocking is never done with any other part of the blade, as this would damage it. Many of the drills focus on attacking the hand with which the opponent is holding the sword.

The jiàn is thought of as a weapon of subtlety and finesse – a scholar's weapon, and thus the evade-and-attack-from-safety principle is of paramount importance.

Traditional and Modern

A number of Tàijí practitioners who have only studied the older traditional Forms feel that the heart of Tàijí has been lost in the modern Forms. Many feel that the modern Forms are often displays of great gymnastic skill, with little of what might be termed 'internal skill'.

Having studied something of both, I think that the potential within both traditional and modern Forms is identical. However, I suspect that the traditional way of teaching Tàijí – which is very repetitive and demanding, which requires great patience, and which *appears* to be a very slow learning process – gives a far better background than the more modern approach. The modern approach though is geared to the modern student who, by and large, wants instant results, and is not prepared to spend the time in getting the basics right.

There are those who complain that Tàijí has become too dance-like, that martial intent has been sacrificed to graceful postures and beautiful movements, that these performers are not grounded, and that one push would send them flying. This is possibly true, but it seems to me that, rather than damaging the art, they benefit it by opening it out to a wider audience; after all, there is no single reason for doing Tàijí, every method has its validity, and there will always be a core of practitioners who understand the traditional methods and build on them.

Perhaps the ideal is to learn a combination of the two, thereby learning a solid grounding, a feeling of the feet initiating movement, the direction of the arm movements controlled from the waist, an upright posture, flexibility in the entire body, grace, and poise.

The Sword Metaphysically

I mention this aspect really for the sake of completeness, because although this book is essentially a textbook of the 32-Posture Sword Form, there are a number of people who have a different viewpoint as to the function of the sword.

The sword can also be thought of as an energetic weapon of both projection and deflection.

A while ago I was teaching a 'pushing swords' exercise (i.e. similar to Pushing Hands but contacting swords instead) and the class had moved to a stage where we were doing the exercise with eyes closed. Working with a student, I suddenly became aware of the difference between the energy emanating from the tip of my partner's sword as he made a slow thrust towards me, and when he made a defensive move.

I then developed this into an exercise where you no longer touch the weapons together, only feel the energy emanating from them. One person would thrust the sword very slowly towards his partner's face, and would then very slowly withdraw it.

As my partner thrust towards me, there was what I can only describe as a very clear and very defined energetic push – 'defined' because it was localized on a small area of my head, and in this respect unlike other experiences of the same type of thing that I have had in the past. When my partner pulled his sword away in the defensive posture, there was a very clear sensation of a vacuum that created a feeling of drawing me towards him.

Whether or not you think that this was just pure imagination, make-believe, or just some arrangement between my partner and myself doesn't really matter; the fact is that the exercise became a sensitivity exercise, and to me felt very real.

Like most things in our world, we can use swordplay on a variety of levels, drawing from it whatever we want. For some the Sword Form can represent a thrust and parry exercise purely on the physical level, for others a graceful dance. For some it might bring a feeling of power and control, for others it's an expression of an aspect of themselves. And for others it becomes the means of an interchange of energy between themselves, the Earth, and the Universe.

The sword therefore becomes a wand. A magician's wand is a long thin crystal of 6–12 inches long that tapers to a point; from the energetic viewpoint, the sword becomes exactly that as it focuses energy at any given part of the blade. Whether magician or swordsman, the skill is in the precision with which you can use the wand/sword. Therefore in a thrust, the energy will be in the tip; in a block, it might be in the third of the blade nearest the handle; in a chop, it will be in the central third of the blade; it is your intention that puts it there.

Intention

Just as in the Hand Forms, the 'intention' of the movement creates and defines the movement; without intention, the movement becomes empty. If you put intention into a movement, you put yourself into it – it serves a purpose. So if you are doing, for example, a chop, it is important to feel as though you are actually chopping something. There are two points here: (1) that you *feel*, and (2) that this does *not* mean that you suddenly do the movement faster.

The intention or feeling makes the energy move through the body, therefore connecting the body from foot to blade, so that the sword actually becomes an extension of *you*. In a very literal sense, it *creates* the movement – it brings it into being and gives it life. To use an analogy, the difference is: one musician who plays a piece of music by only reading the notes, and another who also plays it from the music, but who feels the spirit in which it was written (and therefore plays it from the heart), not only playing those same notes, but also bringing out the emotional content of the music and interpreting the piece.

Development of the 32-Posture Sword Form

A State Sports Committee officially devised this Form in 1957, although in actual fact, its creator was Li Tianji, who then taught it in master classes to instructors around China. Due to the political situation in China at the time, it could not be attributed to one person, and therefore was said to have been devised by a State Sports Committee. Initially it was called the 'Simplified Yang Style Tàijí Sword' Form, and was based on movements from the traditional Yang style Sword Forms. Representative postures and transitions from these Forms were taken and divided into 4 sections of 8 postures per section. The Forms were simplified and standardized, therefore making them easier to teach, whilst, as far as possible, retaining the traditional feel.

It is unclear when the original Forms were created, and the only (rather vague) fact that can be stated is that they developed into their current format towards the end of the 19th century. Many practitioners would like to believe that the Forms are hundreds of years old, and, although it is possible that Tàijí was practised this long ago, there is no historical basis for it.

The popularity of the Form can be attributed to the fact that it was possible to do a set in approximately 3 minutes, and to the fact that music was added.

This original Form had 13 strokes or applications (see below), 7 stances (Bow, Empty, Crouch, One-leg, Feet together, T, Side Bow) and over 10 footwork movements such as step back, step forward, step in, jumping step, turn foot in, turn foot out, various pivots of the foot, etc. Some body movements were also defined (turning, drawing back, etc).

The Opening and Closing Postures (the stepping out at the beginning, and the stepping in at the end) were not included, and as a result, the Opening move in particular, not being a 'textbook' move, is open to a number of variations. Therefore, some teachers start with the feet together, and some with the feet already separated to a shoulder's width apart; some start by turning the palms backward, and others leave them facing inward towards the body.

When performed in competition, however (although it is not a competition Form), it has become more formalized, and there are two firm rules: (1) that in the preparation stance the feet should be together, and (2) that as soon as you move your feet or hands, this signifies the start of the demonstration.

Therefore, this should really be a 34-Posture Sword Form; however, because of the number of years that it has already been in its present format, it will undoubtedly remain known as a 32-Posture Sword Form.

A State Committee laid down rules for swords, which say that the minimum weight of the sword for women is 0–5 kg, and 0–6 kg for men, with no limit for 12 years and under. The sword must be rigid enough so that when the tip is rested on the ground, the blade does not bend.

Since its creation in 1957, the Form has not been altered.

The 13 Applications

The 'applications' (also known as 'techniques') are the methods by which the sword strokes (below) are applied, either in attack or in defence. In other words, the sword has two edges and a tip, and the 'applications' are ways of describing how you use the individual parts of the sword against an opponent.

For example, the application **diǎn** (dot, point, etc.) is to use only the tip in a downward movement against the opponent (usually the wrist or hand), whereas the application **pī** (chop) is to use the middle third of the blade against the body or limb of the opponent. A further example would be **dài**, which is to use the whole length of the blade against e.g. the torso, drawing the blade across the body from hilt to tip.

In this Form, there are 13 main sword applications or techniques, some of which are for defence, some for attack, and some for simultaneous defence and attack; they are **diǎn, cì, sǎo, dài, pī, chōu, liāo, lán, guà, jié, tuō, jī, mǒ**.

The number 13 is considered very lucky amongst martial artists; possibly this is because of the combination of the numbers in the 5 Elements and the 8 Hexagrams (changes).

The Form is organized so that, in most cases (but not all), the final posture of each of the 32 Postures of the Form is the application, but in fact, there are intermediate applications throughout in the connecting movements.

The most common applications or techniques in the 32-Posture Sword Form are **cì** (thrust), **pī** (chop), and **dài** (draw/carry).

CHAPTER

2

Techniques

Sword Strokes

Sword Strokes in Section 1

点 = diǎn

(pron. "dee-en")
dot; point; poke; jab; strike at a vital point.

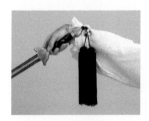

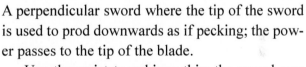

A perpendicular sword where the tip of the sword is used to prod downwards as if pecking; the power passes to the tip of the blade.

Use the wrist to achieve this; the sword arm plays relatively little part in the stroke. The sword is mainly supported by the index and middle fingers; the other three fingers are relaxed. This connection of hand and sword therefore acts as a pivotal point so that the sword can move freely; it is important not to grip too tightly. This is not a large movement of the sword, but is usually quite a quick one. The purpose of **diǎn** is to attack an opponent's wrist, hand, or fingers of the arm that is holding the sword.

Tiǎo is not one of the 13 applications, but should be mentioned as the movement appears at this point in the order of applications in the 32-Posture Sword Form, in the moves leading into Posture 2.

挑 = **tiǎo**

(pron. "tee-ow" as in 'now')
carry on a pole.

A vertical sword, letting the sword tip rise upwards like a carrying pole; the power is in the front part of the blade.

The tip of the sword thrusts at an opponent, possibly piercing the skin, and then cuts rapidly upward with a flick of the wrist. There is no arm movement; the entire action is performed by the flexion of the wrist.

刺 = **cì**

(pron. "tsir")
thrust; stab; prick; poke.

Thrusting the tip of the sword rapidly and powerfully straight at an opponent, the arm being extended from a bent position and making a straight line with the sword.

The power extends to the tip of the sword; if the blade-edges face left and right, it is a flat thrust (*píng*cìjiàn); if the blade-edges face up and down, it is a perpendicular thrust (*lì*cìjiàn). The thrust can be directed upward, downward, forward, backward, sideways, or overhead in an inverted thrust. The power of the thrust comes from the back leg combined with the

turn of the waist. Once you have committed to this movement, it can leave you open to a counter-attack, should you miss your target.

扫 = sǎo

(pron. "sow" as in 'now')
sweep.

A flat sword brandished and swung from left side to right side, or vice versa.

The arm and the sword make a straight line; the power is in the middle third of the blade-edge. The cut is often to the wrist, leg, or ankle. The height of **sǎo** is anywhere below the shoulders. This is a scything action.

带 = dài

(pron. "dye")
belt; girdle; carry; bring; take back.

A flat sword drawn or whipped from the front backwards to the side.

The power point is usually in the length of the blade-edge as a smooth movement, but it can also be in the tip (an attack to your opponent's wrist), or in the ridge of the blade (adhering to your opponent's blade). This is often thought of as 'carry back', as in 'draw back', or even 'slice back' (across the opponent's body), and involves the turn of the waist, and the flexing of the wrist. In other words, it is the full length of the blade-edge being drawn across your opponent's body or limb.

The movement is usually performed by extending the arm first, with the tip of the sword leading away from you, then rotating the body to left or right with the arm fairly well extended. Therefore keep the right elbow fairly open. (An analogy of this is to imagine a bicycle wheel lying on its side – the hub of the wheel is your centre. You extend the right arm (one of the spokes), and then rotate your centre so that the sword follows the outer movement of the rim (tyre) of the wheel.) This is the horizontal equivalent of **chōu** (see below).

劈 = pī

(pron. "peee")
chop; hack; split open.

A perpendicular sword coming forcefully downwards from above. The power is in the middle section of the blade-edge, and, at the moment of contact in the chop, both arm and sword form a straight line. **Lūn pī** means to describe a big circle first and then chop. The movement can be initiated from high up on either your left or your right side. The chop finishes either parallel to the ground, or with the blade angled downward at 45°.

抽 = chōu

(pron. "cho" as in 'go')
lash; whip; draw out; extract; pull; take out; draw along; draw back (like pulling a draw out of a chest of drawers, or drawing a letter from an envelope).

26

A perpendicular sword drawn or whipped back towards the body, with either an upward or a downward *arc*. The point of power is either in (approximately) the centre of the blade-edge, in the length of the blade-edge, or in the centre of the ridge depending upon whether the stroke is used for attack or for defence. For example, the edge of the blade, if placed under a limb, would be pulled back to make a cut, whereas the centre of the ridge of the blade could also be used to block a thrust.

This stroke is often thought of as 'draw back' or 'pull back' like **dài**, and the principles of **dài** apply to **chōu**; but in **chōu**, the sword blade is perpendicular. This stroke is not just used to attack; it also adopts the idea of neutralization.

In this Form, **chōu** appears three times, (Postures 7, 17, and 30), twice with an inverted perpendicular blade (Postures 7 and 30) in which the cutting or working edge of the sword is the upper one (an upward arc). In Posture 17, **chōu** occurs with the cutting or working edge of the blade being the lower one (a downward arc). This is the vertical equivalent of **dài** (see above).

The above six techniques appear in Section 1 and are repeated throughout the other three sections.

Sword Strokes in Section 2

截 = jié

(pron. "jee-air")
cut off (e.g. a length of something); intercept; block; separate into pieces *(e.g. the concept of a dam across a river)*. You use the centre of the sword to 'divide' an object.

Cutting with a perpendicular sword or flat sword to parry and intercept the opponent. The power is in the blade-edge at the point of contact; if blocking another weapon, the bluntest third of the blade nearest the hilt is used, but it is better to use the sharper edge of the blade to block (cut) an opponent's sword arm or wrist, having evaded his attack. This should not be confused with **chōu** (in which the blade might be drawn backward as though 'slicing' using the length of the blade); this is a 'pressing' of the blade (e.g. downward).

APPLICATION NOTES:

Jié can be used downward, upward, forward, or from one side to the other. You can use **jié** downward on to an opponent's wrist, upward under an opponent's arm to attack his wrist, forward if he attacks using (e.g.) **dài**, or from the side:

E.g. Your opponent uses **pī** (chop) to your head; side-step to avoid the chop and then use **jié** to the side of his wrist using the centre of the blade with your sword vertical.

Pěng is not one of the 13 applications, but should be mentioned as the movement appears at this point in the order of applications in the 32-Posture Sword Form, in the moves leading into Posture 13.

捧 = pěng

(pron. "pung" as in 'lung')
hold/offer with both hands.

Supporting a perpendicular or flat sword with both hands in front of the body as if making an offering; same as 抱 **bào** *(pron. as in 'cow')* but **pěng** is usual.

撩 = liāo

(pron. "lee-ow" as in 'now')
lift up (e.g. a curtain); sprinkle; slide upward.

Lifting upwards and away from the body with a perpendicular sword, the sword moving from behind you to ahead of you.

The power point is in the front part of the blade-edge; lift the tip of the blade upwards and forwards up an opponent's body. The blade can move from the left or right side of the body.

Sword Strokes in Section 3

拦 = lán

(pron. "lan" as in 'man')
block; stop; break off midway; hinder; obstruct.

A perpendicular sword with the tip pointing diagonally downwards, and the action of the blade facing forward and up in a lifting action. In the final posture, the hand holding the sword can be as high as eye height, and the tip of the sword should be approximately at waist height.

The power point is in the middle and rear part of the blade. It is the deflection of an opponent's thrust by sliding his sword to the side, away from your body. Using **lán**, the sword acts like a shield to protect you, or to block an attack. It is a 'lifting block', and can appear to be very similar to **liāo**, but **lán** is a blocking not a cutting technique. In **liāo** the tip of the sword points directly away from you (straight ahead), but in **lán**, the blade is angled at 45° to your body, and therefore points to either the left or right forward diagonal. It also differs from **liāo** in that the blade is diagonal to the direction of your opponent; in **liāo**, the tip will point at your opponent.

Chuān is not one of the 13 applications, but should be mentioned as the movement appears at this point in the order of applications in the Form, in the moves leading into Posture 22.

穿 = chuān

(pron. "choo-an")
penetrate; bore through; thread.

A flat or perpendicular sword penetrating outwards in a different direction along the leg, arm, or body; the arm straightens out from a bent position; the power point is in the tip of the sword. The movement involves a turn of the body often of 180° or more, and can be seen as a method of converting a defensive move (to an attack coming from behind) into an attack (usually **cì**).

Sword Strokes in Section 4

The following two strokes need to be mentioned together, as they are virtually identical and the teachers seem to differ in their explanantions as to why they are called by different names. Some say that they differ only in the direction the tip points, but others say that the function is slightly different for each, as explained below.

托 = tuō

(pron. "tour" as in 'more')
hold in the palm; support from underneath.

A perpendicular sword lifted upwards to past head height; the power is in the blade-edge (same as **jià** but the sword points to your right). This is a horizontal upward block, often with the thicker section of the blade nearer the hilt.

Some teachers say that **tuō** is one blade lifting another blade, i.e. the two blades are in contact and the lower one pushes up under the upper one.

架 = jià

(pron. "jee-ah")
put up; erect; support (as of a shelf); ward off.

A perpendicular sword lifted upwards to past head height; the power is in the blade-edge (same as **tuō** but the sword points to your left). This stroke follows the same principle as **lán** but the block is above the head. It is a horizontal upward block, often with the thicker section of the blade nearer the hilt.

Some teachers say that **jià** is a vertical lift of the blade, which, unlike **tuō** is *not* in conflict with the other blade, or limbs, above it. So it is a forceful vertical lift *into* the oponent's weapon or limb.

挂 = guà

(pron. "gwar")
hang (something); suspend.

The sword tip is hooked backwards either upward or downward, from front to back, with a perpendicular blade, to keep the opponent away as he advances to attack, or to divert his attack. In effect, you hook your sword either downward or upward with the tip leading, so that the faces (sides) brush his weapon aside. The energy is therefore in the face of the body of the sword.

Jiǎo is not one of the 13 applications, but should be mentioned as the movement appears at this point in the order of applications in the 32-Posture Sword Form, in the moves leading into Posture 25.

绞 = jiǎo *(pron. "jee-ow" as in 'now')*
twist; stir; mix.

A flat sword, letting the sword tip go clockwise or anti-clockwise as if describing a small vertical or horizontal circle in a twisting motion. The energy to the blade is produced, not by the wrist, but by the turn of the body.

击 = jī *(pron. "jee")*
hit; strike (e.g. a bell); throw (e.g. a stone); hammer (something); attack; bump into.

A flat sword flicked towards left or right; attacking towards the right is also called a flat **bēng** 崩 stroke. The energy is released in a rapid movement by the forearm, and passes through the sword to the front edge of the tip, which arrives last. This can be an attack to an opponent's wrist, or throat.

Jī, **diǎn**, and **bēng** have similarities. **Jī** is to 'flick' with the tip (usually diagonally upwards as though across the face), **diǎn** is to use the tip on a downward vertical line (from above to below as though to attack the wrist by dropping the tip downwards – like drawing a full stop with a pencil), **bēng** is to use the tip on an upward vertical line (usually from below to above – e.g. as though flicking the tip up under someone's chin). In the 42-Posture Sword Form and in the Wudang Tàijí Sword Form, the **jī** is done with power, but in the 32-Posture Sword Form (and in the 16-Posture Sword Form) it is done with a gentle consistent movement.

31

抹 = mǒ

(pron. "more")
wipe; smear.

A flat sword as if led across the neck from left to right or right to left; the power point follows the sword blade-edge in a smooth movement. This is a circling cut, and can be easily confused with **dài** or **sǎo**.

It is arguable that the following three 'applications' can also be found in the Form, although they are not part of the 13 applications. These possible applications are mentioned in the text at the relevant point, but are marked in a border (as below).

tándiǎn 镡点	means to point, hit, or poke with jiàntán, the tassel holder. The sword is held in the left hand in the reversed position (as at the start of the Form), and the tassel holder is used to strike the opponent.
jiànbǐng lángé 剑柄拦格	means to use jiànbǐng 剑柄, the handle of the sword, to block the opponent's attack. The jiàn is held in the left hand in the reversed position (as at the start of the Form).
Juédiǎn 决点	means to use jiànjué, the finger sword, to attack the opponent. Energy, qì, moves to the fingertips, strengthening them. This 'application' involves attacking vital acupuncture points with the fingers.

32

Originally all 13 techniques came under four headings:

jī	击	flick
cì	刺	thrust
gé	格	slice
xǐ	洗	block

Stances (步形 Bùxíng)

弓步 gōngbù

1. Bow stance

BRIEF:
One foot ahead of the other, with 70% weight on the front foot; the front knee bent, the back leg naturally straightened.

In order to get into a Bow stance, stand with your feet a shoulder's width apart and with both feet pointing straight ahead. Turn your right foot outwards to 45°, and then, with your weight on your right foot, and bending your right knee, move your left foot *directly* ahead (as though sliding it parallel to the side walls of a room). Don't allow the foot to move to the right as you move it forwards, and it is *very* important to keep the toes pointing straight ahead. Next, move 70% of your weight on to the left foot, keeping both feet flat on the ground.

This is a left Bow stance. As mentioned before, the toes of the left foot *must* point straight ahead; the toes of the right foot pointing outwards at 45°. The left knee is bent forwards like a bow so that it is vertically above the toes; the right leg is extended straight and naturally.

The width between your heels *laterally* is determined by the posture, but is usually anything from 4–12 inches. For example, if you are in a right Bow stance (with the right foot forwards), and you are thrusting with the sword (i.e. with your right hand), this will tend to be a narrower stance because the arm and leg on the same side of the body are forwards. A left Bow stance with the same right-handed thrust will have a wider stance.

The weight distribution is usually 70/30, but can also be found as 60/40.

34

A note on the 'straightening' of the back leg: The rear leg *is* bent, but the bend is achieved by the relaxation/release of the pelvis, rather than by bending the actual knee. To get the feel of it, go into the posture described above and then lock the rear leg. Next, try relaxing the pelvis particularly around the area of the sacrum, and the rear leg will bend slightly, but in the same way that an archer's bow will bend.

侧弓步 cègōngbù

2. Side Bow stance

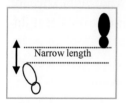

Narrow length

Whereas an ordinary Bow stance is greater in length than in width, a Side Bow stance is greater in width than in length.

Starting with the feet together, turn your right toes 45° to the right, and then step sideways with (e.g.) the left foot; but instead of stepping directly sideways to 9.00 (see page 48 for explanation of the 'clock' directions), step towards 10.00 with the heel. Place the heel, and point the toes to 12.00. (The *width* of the stance is the amount that you step out to your left; the amount that you move the left foot forwards (i.e. to 10.00) is the *length* of the stance.) In the final posture, if you imagine a thick line of about 4–8 inches (10–20 centimetres) width, drawn from 9.00 to 3.00 between your feet, the heel of your right foot should be against one side of the line, and the toes of the left foot should be against the other side of the line. The toes of the left foot point to 12.00, and the toes of the right foot point to about 1.30.

仆步 púbù

3. Crouching stance (like a servant)

Stand with both feet together (with your back to a wall in order to get the angle of the feet correct in the posture), and about 12 inches away from the wall; your toes point to 12.00.

(a) Turn the toes of your (for example) right foot outward by 30–45°, and move your weight on to your right foot.

(b) Lift up your left foot, and touch the toes against the back of the heel of your right foot (this is in order to get the line of the left foot accurately in the following movement). Next, keeping your weight completely on your right foot, slide your left foot sideways along an imaginary line that starts at your right heel, and which is parallel to the wall (in other words, your left heel will lightly brush along the wall). As you do this, sink down into your right heel, bending your right knee as much as possible. Keep the right knee over the right toes, and keep the soles of both feet flat on the ground. The tip of your spine – your coccyx – should be as directly above your right heel as possible.

(c) To move out of a Crouching stance, as your weight moves forward on to your left foot, turn your left foot outward so that the toes point to 9.00, then (d) turn the toes of your right foot to point to 10.30, pivoting on the *heel*.

a

b

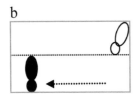

c

d

虚步 **xūbù**

4. Empty stance

Stand with both feet together. Turn the toes of your (for example) right foot outwards by 30–45°, and move your weight on to your right foot. Bending your right knee, move your left foot as far ahead of you as possible, putting the foot flat on the floor with no weight on it. The left foot can also have only the toes/ball of the foot touching the floor, or the toes can be raised with only the heel on the floor.

丁步 **dīngbù**

5. T-stance

Stand with both feet together. Turn the toes of your (for example) right foot outwards by 30–45°, and move your weight on to your right foot. Bending your right knee, lift the left heel; there should be no weight on the left toes. (Dīng in Chinese is a 'nail'. Not only does the character for the word closely resemble a nail, but the way in which the foot is held in this stance also copies the shape of a nail – with the toe touching the ground.)

37

坐盘步
zuòpánbù

6a. Sitting stance

Stand with both feet together. Step straight ahead with your right foot, and, as you place your right heel, turn the toes of your right foot outwards by 45°. As you move your weight on to your right foot, bend your right knee and turn your torso to your right. As you do so, gently press your inner thighs together, and, bending your left knee also, allow the lateral side (the outside) of your left knee to touch the lateral side (the outside) of your right calf. The right foot is flat on the ground, but the left heel is raised off the floor. Ideally, the buttocks should be close to the rear heel in this semi-squatting posture, but the posture can be done at varying heights depending upon the agility of the practitioner.

38

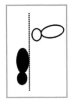

半坐盘步
bànzuòpánbù

6b. Half-sitting stance

To do this, turn your body to the right, and gently press the *outside* of the left thigh – just above the left knee – against the *outside* of your right calf, and raise your left heel (i.e. the knees will be crossed). Pressing the legs together will help your stability, as well as putting less strain on the knees. The weight will either be distributed evenly between both feet, or will be slightly more on the front foot.

独立步 **dúlìbù**

7. One-legged stance

With feet together, turn one foot outward by 30–45° and move your weight on to it. (In this posture, there is no need to bend the supporting leg.) Lift the other leg up as high as possible with a relaxed calf (i.e. just lift up the knee). Stylistically, in some of the one-legged 32-Sword Postures, the knee should point out to the side slightly, although in others the knee should point straight ahead in the direction in which you are about to step. The sole of the raised foot should be turned in to become as parallel as possible to the thigh of the supporting leg (i.e. as straight a line as possible from knee to toes). The *minimum* requirement is that the thigh is parallel to the ground. The supporting leg should be straight, but not locked.

开立步 **kàilìbù**

8. Standing with feet apart

This is the basic 'shoulder-width stance'. The 'perfect' shoulder-width stance is measured as follows, and will be very slightly different for every person:

Stand with feet together, and, temporarily moving your weight on to your heels, turn both feet outwards to exactly 45°. Next, move your weight back on to your toes, and lifting your heels, square them up to parallel again. By doing this, the outside edges of your feet are directly below the outside edges of your shoulders, and the inside edges of your feet are directly below the axillary creases – the lines of the armpits.

Footwork (步法 bùfǎ)

Examples of the footwork techniques are:

上步 shàngbù

Forward step
The rear leg is moved forward one step, or the front leg is moved half a step forwards.

退步 tuìbù

Backward step (E.g. Posture 7)
The front leg is moved back one step.

撤步 chèbù

Withdrawing step (E.g. Posture 28)
The front leg or the rear leg is moved back half a step.

扣步 kòubù

Turning-in step (E.g. Posture 31)
As the foot comes down after a forward step, the foot is placed on the ground so that the feet form a Chinese figure eight shape / \.

摆步 bǎibù

Swing step (E.g. moving into Postures 22 (first move); 26 (first move); 29 (second move))
As the foot comes down on the ground after a forward step, the heel is placed first and then the toes are turned outwards and placed on the ground so that the feet form an outward Chinese figure eight shape \ /.

跳步 tiàobù

Jump step (E.g. Posture 14)
Pressing the front foot on the ground and jumping up from there, the rear leg swinging forwards and landing on a foot which is turned outwards and placed on the ground so that the feet form an outward Chinese figure eight shape \ /.

碾步 niǎnbù

Grinding step (E.g. the right foot at the end of moving into the first Bow stance)
With the heel as an axis, the toes are turned outwards or inwards; or with the ball of the foot as an axis, the heel is turned out.

40

The Sword-Fingers (劍指 **jiàn zhǐ**)

The index and middle fingers are extended and held together; the little and ring fingers are curled, and the tip of the thumb rests on the first joints of both (i.e. rest the pad of the thumb on the nails).

There is another way to hold the sword-fingers, perhaps less common. The index and middle fingers are extended in the usual way, but the ring and little fingers are curled very tightly so that the tips touch the palm at the root of the fingers. The thumb is then bent very strongly so that the thumbnail actually pushes firmly against the nails of the two fingers.

This way of holding the left hand has a very different feel to the softer way described previously; it is a more 'yang' method, more aggressive, and in some ways balances out the hardness of the sword. There is a completely different feel to the energy of the Form when holding the hand in this manner.

Also worth mentioning is that the sword-fingers in Sun style Tàijí are held slightly differently. In this style, the thumb, little, and ring fingers are not connected; whilst the index and middle fingers are held together and extended as usual, the little and ring fingers are bent inward, but the thumb is extended outward to the side, either straight out to the side, or slightly bent inward.

There are various names for this hand position such as 'sword-fingers', 'sword-hand', 'secret sword', 'sword amulet', or 'sword charm'.

The left 'sword-fingers' are used only with the double-edged sword; with the sabre (**dāo**), for example, a palm is used. The outstretched arm has the function of balancing the sword, but in certain cases is also to add to the aesthetic, or visual quality of the posture. The reason for the actual hand shape is a point of discussion, and some instructors teach that it can be used to press, or thrust at, vital acupuncture points. Perhaps this is correct – it is not a technique that I have been taught, but the main reason for the particular hand position is a non-functional one and lies in Daoist history and philosophy.

The hand shape has a close connection to Daoism, and was used as a 'talisman', or 'amulet'. In Daoist philosophy, it is felt that pressing the fingers together in certain ways can aid communication with the Heavens, as an energetic circuit is completed within the body. This is also true in some meditation practices, and in some Daoist practices it is often the tips of the middle finger and thumb that are placed together.

It is also worth mentioning at this point that the double-edged sword itself is considered a holy weapon that can, amongst other things, be used against demons. It was the preferred weapon of the Daoist monks, whereas Buddhist monks preferred the sabre.

The origins of the sword-fingers are related in the legend of Zhūgě Liàng who 'borrowed the East wind'.

The Legend of Zhūgě Liàng (诸葛亮)

Zhūgě Liàng (A.D. 181–234) was a man who was famous for his ability to 'borrow the East wind'.

At this time, China was divided into three different countries; North of the Yangxe was one large country, and South of the Yangxe, the land was divided into two smaller countries.

The North had a vast army, skilled at warfare particularly on horseback, and they decided to invade the two Southern countries.

The main problem that the North faced was that their army was inexperienced at warfare on water, and in order to invade, their army had to cross the Yangxe River, fending off any naval attacks from the South in the process.

The North were also concerned that seasickness would make their soldiers unable to fight, and to avoid this, and in an attempt to make the boats as stable and as much like fighting on land as possible, they decided to link their boats together into a vast platform.

The two countries South of the Yangxe, upon discovering this plan, realized that, as all the boats were connected together, they would be much easier to burn. They prepared as many small boats as they could, loading them with wood and oil with the intention of sending them in amongst and around the Northern army's 'boat platform'.

However, there was a problem: it was winter, and in winter the wind blows from the North, from Mongolia; it was therefore blowing in the wrong direction. They needed an Easterly wind not only to drive their own ships toward the enemy's platform, but also to fan the flames from one side of the 'boat platform' to the other.

It was then that Zhūgě Liàng, a military advisor to the government, proposed that he 'borrow' the wind and alter its direction for three days. He requested that a tall platform be built for him, and that under no circumstance should he be disturbed in his meditation for three days.

Zhūgě Liàng climbed to his platform, and, for three days, he meditated, holding his sword in one hand, and holding his other hand in the shape of the sword-fingers. On the third day, the wind changed direction.

An Easterly wind arose, and the Southern fireboats were launched. They were guided towards the 'boat platform', which caught fire and rapidly burnt. For three days the wind blew, fanning the flames and killing over a million soldiers; only eighty were left to protect the retreating general.

Legend has it that this took place 2000 years ago, during the peak of the Daoist Period.

In those days, much was determined by the beliefs of the emperor, and, because Zhūgě Liàng was a Daoist, this episode served to strengthen both Buddhism and Daoism.

Method of Raising the Left Sword-Fingers

The movement that occurs most regularly for the left arm and sword-fingers is to circle them from the left side of the waist, out to the left side of the body, and then up above the head.

I will use Posture 19 as an example. As this movement occurs so often, it is worth describing the movement in some detail.

The hand often starts with the left sword-fingers on the left side of the waist with the palm turned up. Keeping the arm as rounded as possible, open the arm out to the left side, leading sideways with the back of the hand, gradually pointing the sword-fingers to the ground, and allowing the arm to gently stretch, almost as though it is unwinding. As the arm becomes parallel to the ground, begin to lift the sword-fingers so that they point to the side; the left

The left sword-fingers start to lower with the right wrist, but then separate to move palm up to the left side of the waist.

44

The left sword-fingers move from the waist, out to the left side, to rise level with or above the head.

palm should now be facing the ground. Let the fingertips arrive last like the tip of a whip.

The hand continues to lift, but now with the tips of the sword-fingers leading the arm, and the left wrist slowly flexing backward.

The arm should finish with the left palm facing the ceiling, the arm in a graceful arc, and the sword-fingers pointing towards your front right. The actual angle of the raised arm varies from move to move, depending upon angles of the rest of the body.

The most important point of all is to relax the left shoulder when going into this position, so that the arm is lifted from the shoulder joint only. This is the most common mistake when teaching Sword Forms.

- Avoid leading the left arm with the elbow.

- Avoid taking the arm or elbow behind the back; the shoulder blade should not be pulled inward toward the spine.

General Note about the Left Sword-Fingers

In the postures at the end of each Form, the *palm* of the left hand is usually *down* when close to the wrist of the hand holding the sword, palm up when 'wiping' the waist, or facing away from the body in all other positions. There are two Postures where the left sword-fingers 'support' the right hand from underneath (with palm up) – Postures 13 and 18, although this can also be done with an 'open' hand.

Definitions of Terms Used

The Clock System of Defining Directions

The usual method of defining directions in Tàijí is the compass points, and normally this assumes a starting direction of South. This works moderately well, but runs into problems when you need to describe a 30° turn from one of the cardinal points.

I have therefore used the clock system as opposed to the compass points, as I think it is easier to understand. The clock system always refers to the hour hand, and assumes that you start with the body facing 12 o'clock (12.00). A 90° turn to your right will therefore take you to 3 o'clock (3.00), and a further 45° turn will take you to 4.30, etc.

The clock system has the added advantage of easily defining 30° turns, as every hour is at 30°.

Terms Used to Describe the Positioning of the Blade

The edges of the blade will be referred to as the 'upper edge' and the 'lower edge'. The sides of the blade will be referred to as the left and right 'faces'.

- **Flat/Horizontal sword** – (平劍 píngjiàn)
  A flat sword (blade); the sword is held so that, if the whole sword rested on the ground, the faces, or sides, of the blade would be parallel to the ground.

- **Perpendicular/Vertical sword** – (立劍 lìjiàn)

A perpendicular sword (blade); the sword is held so that, if the whole sword were rested on the ground, the blade would be perpendicular to the ground, as if the entire length of the blade were cutting into the ground.

The Sword-Fingers

The Sword-Fingers are also known as Sword-Hand, Secret Sword, Sword-Amulet or Sword-Charm. This hand position will be referred to throughout this book as 'sword-fingers' or 'sword-hand'.

'Slipping the (rear) heel'

When moving into certain postures, it is necessary to adjust the rear foot, so that the two feet do not form an angle of 90°.

In Tàijí, there are two ways of doing this, either by lifting the toes of the rear foot, and turning them inward by 45° (this is the 'traditional' way), or by leaving the toes in place, and pushing the heel backward by 45° (this is the 'modern' way).

Both have their merits, but in the 32-Posture Sword Form, the latter method is used more often than the former.

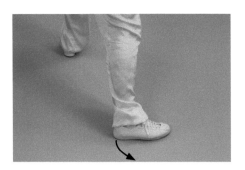 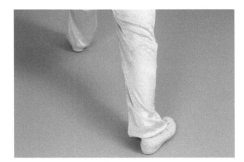

'Primary' and 'Secondary' Applications

There are 13 'Primary Applications', which usually define each of the Postures (see page 21). These are the applications around which the Sword Form is designed, and which need to be understood to be the 'main' applications of the Form. Were you to perform this Sword Form in a competition, you would need to demonstrate that you understood this to be the case. In music it would be the equivalent of phrases within the piece; in writing it is the equivalent of punctuation marks and sentence structure.

The remainder, 'Secondary Applications', are suggestions for other applications *within* the connecting movements. You will sometimes find these in the middle of the text alongside the Posture to which they are relevant, which might even be in the middle of an individual Posture. They are only suggestions, and are most definitely *not* the textbook applications of the Form.

The Kua

This is the area between the pelvis and the upper thigh; the diagonal 'crease' leading from the outer pelvis to the crotch; or the join where the leg meets the body/pelvis. Anatomically this is the 'inguinal groove'.

In dance, or in ballet, the ability to open the thigh outward to the side whilst keeping the pelvis facing the front would be called 'turn out'. It is very easy to forget to relax this part of the body, which locks the thighs and makes the movements of the lower body rather rigid.

The 'Centre', 'Centre-turn', and the 'Centreline' of the body

The 'centre' refers to the Dantien, 1–2 inches below the navel, and approximately a third inwards towards the centre of the body. 'Centre-turn' or the expression 'turning your centre' refers to the way in which you turn this core of the body.

The 'centreline' of the body simply refers to a line that equates with the Ren channel (Conception Vessel) running down the front of the body. It is used to describe which way the body is facing. (See also the additional information at the end in Chapter 5 'Beyond the Basics'.)

Key to Footprint Diagrams

Left Foot   =   [●●]   Black and dotted line   e.g.   ······▶

Right Foot   =   [○○]   White and solid line   e.g.   ──────▶

The arrow, depending upon its positioning, refers either to the direction of the next step, or to where the foot has come from.

The triangle ▽ or ▲ signifies toes down or toes up, and the colour again refers to right (white) or left (black).

'Slipping the heel' is shown by a thicker arrow which starts from the heel. It is a black arrow for the left foot (⬆) and a white for the right foot (⇧).

'Turning the toes' is shown by a short arrow: Either ⋯▶ (left) or ⟶ (right).

CHAPTER **3**

The Form

Each Posture of the Form will be introduced in the formula shown in the boxes below. This will be followed by a more detailed breakdown of the Posture into its component moves.

Posture Number	English (Traditional name of Posture)	English (Modern name of Posture)
	Chinese Pinyin	Chinese Pinyin
	Chinese Characters	Chinese Characters

Opening the Form

The sword is initially held in the left hand as follows: The ring, middle, and little fingers support the underside of one side of the guard, and the thumb is under the other side. The index finger runs down the length of the hilt.

The majority of Sword Forms start with the left hand holding the sword. This is just a tradition;

nowadays there are also Forms starting with the right hand holding the sword.

It is not part of the competition rules that all Sword Forms should begin with the sword held in the left hand.

Initial Stance

BRIEF:
Feet together. The posture is upright.

DETAILS:
The body faces 12.00. Both arms hang naturally at the side of the body. The left hand holds the sword, the blade of which is against the back of the left arm; the left palm faces backward.

The right hand is held in the sword-fingers position, with the palm facing your body.

The eyes look forward.

NOTES:

- Allow the neck to lengthen; this has the effect of allowing the chin to 'tuck under' without your having to force it under. Avoid the sword touching the body or resting in the crease of the armpit.

C	Three Halos Around the Moon (Lit. Encase the Moon with Three Rings)	Commence (Lit. Starting Posture)
	sānhuán tàoyuě	qǐ shì
	三环套月	起势

'Three halos around the moon': There are various explanations for this name. (1) Because there are three steps involved in the movement. (2) I have also heard it explained that the name comes from the three circles that the hands make – a right-handed and a left-handed one simultaneously at the start of the Form, and another one with the right hand before the **diǎn** of Posture 1. However, the best (or perhaps most appealing) explanation that I've come across is that (3) there are three 'defensive' circles formed during this opening sequence (a) by the left hand at the start of the Posture (see moves 3–5 below), (b) by both the left and right hands connecting (move 6 below), and (c) again by both the left and right hands connecting (move 8 below). Apparently the reason for this is that the jiàn is very much considered the 'gentleman's weapon', and as such, the gentleman would give his attacker/opponent three attempts to attack him before he retaliated; the first three movements are therefore defensive, followed by Posture 1 (**diǎn**), which is the first attack.

C.1

BRIEF:
Step sideways a shoulders' width with the left foot.

DETAILS:
When stepping out, the knees are *not* bent. Move the weight over the right foot allowing the body to elongate and the crown therefore to rise (relax the neck). This will free the left foot, which can be moved sideways. As you do so, turn the right and left palms to face backward.

NOTES:

- You can also move both arms sideways and slightly away from the body; but this is not a textbook requirement, and is therefore not obligatory.

C.2

BRIEF:

Raise the hands ahead of you.

DETAILS:

Raise the hilt of the sword and the right sword-fingers to shoulder height, both palms still down. Keep the shoulders relaxed and the head level.

When doing so, allow the arms to lengthen at the elbow joint, so that the hands extend away from you. The elbows are relaxed, and slightly opened out to the sides. The legs remain straight. The eyes look straight ahead.

NOTES:

- As you raise the hands, allow the shoulders to relax and sink.

- When the hands have risen, the tip of the sword will point slightly downward.

C.3

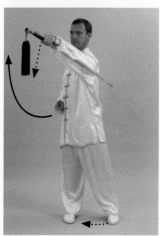

BRIEF:
Circle the sword to your right.

DETAILS:
Move your weight on to your right foot, and turn your body slightly to the right (approximately 1.00). Simultaneously, raise the sword up to forehead height (or slightly higher) and then circle it to your right.

Meanwhile, your right sword-fingers, with palm turning up, circle down your centreline to the right side of your waist.

NOTES:

• The eyes follow the left hand, but without looking up.

As you sink into the right foot, draw the left toes into the right foot, not touching the floor, and simultaneously the right sword-fingers rise (palm turning up) to shoulder height at 1.30. As the right hand rises, the left hand, holding the sword, lowers with palm down, to opposite the sternum breastbone. The body has turned slightly left again (approximately 12.00), and the eyes look beyond the right hand.

NOTES:

• Make a generous circle up and to the right with the left hand.

• The sword is still 'attached' under the left forearm, with the blade angled less than 45° to the ground.

• Think of the right fingers as a continuation of the hilt of the sword, i.e. as a straight line.

C.4

BRIEF:
Fold the right hand, push the left hand down, and place the left foot.

DETAILS:
Step out wide to 9.00 with the left heel, as the hilt of the sword sweeps down your centreline to in front of the inside of your left thigh (the blade is still behind your left forearm and the tip will therefore rise), and your right sword-fingers move to outside your right ear. The weight is still on the right foot, and the left toes are raised. The body has now turned more so that the centreline is facing approximately 10.30.

NOTES:

- This is a not unlike the intermediate position of a 'Brush Knee and Side Step' in the Hand Forms.

- Avoid making the stance too narrow when you step. The width should be about 12 inches (30 centimetres) apart.

- Avoid allowing the right sword-fingers to 'collapse'; keep a very slight curve from the right elbow to the right fingertips.

- Relax the right shoulder and elbow.

- Keep the weight on the back foot as you place the left foot; avoid 'falling' into the front foot.

Jiànbǐng lángé 剑柄拦格 means to use jiànbǐng, the handle of the sword, to block the opponent's attack. The jiàn is held in the left hand in the reversed position (as at the start of the Form).

C.5

Alt. view

BRIEF:
Transfer the weight forward, move your right hand ahead, and your sword to your side.

DETAILS:
Move your weight on to your left foot and continue to bring the hilt of the sword down so that the blade is vertical by your left side and behind your left forearm. Meanwhile the right sword-fingers extend to 9.00, initially with the fingertips leading, and finally, as the hand arrives in position, the wrist flexes so that the fingers become vertical. As you arrive in the final position, slip the rear heel.

NOTES:

- This is very similar to the finishing posture of 'Brush Knee and Side Step'.

- The end of the first 'Halo Around the Moon'.

SECONDARY APPLICATION NOTES:
Moves 4 and 5 could be seen as a block downward of your opponent's sword to your left, followed by a thrust of the left sword-fingers to his throat.

55

Juédiǎn 决点 means to use jiànzhǐ, the sword-fingers, to attack the opponent.

Energy, qì, is passed to the fingertips, thereby strengthening them. This 'application' involves attacking vital acupuncture points with the fingers. However, note that, in the Posture, the fingers are vertical.

C.6

Alt.
view

BRIEF:
Extend the right fingers and bend the left elbow; turn right palm as you cross-step; cross the hilt over your wrist.

DETAILS:
Move your weight over your left foot, and, as you do so, point your right fingers forwards. Simultaneously, bend your left elbow, thus lifting the hilt of the sword from being by your left side to point to 9.00 (with the blade still lying along the underside of your arm).

Turn your right palm upwards (still holding the sword-fingers) and step to 9.00 with your right heel (toes turned out to a minimum of 10.30). Push the pommel and hilt of the sword (palm down) over your right wrist (there is a feeling of 'threading' it over the wrist), which is drawing back (palm up) to your waist.

NOTES:

- Avoid stepping too far ahead with the right foot.

- Be aware of the circular connection within the arms – possibly the second 'Halo...'.

SECONDARY APPLICATION NOTES:
Although this is not one of the 13 applications, this movement and the following movement could possibly be thought of as a strike with the tassel holder, and/or a block with either the face of the blade (to the left), or with the handle of the sword.

Tándiǎn 镡点 means to point, hit, or poke with 'jiàntán', the tassel holder.

The sword is held in the left hand in the reversed position (as at the start of the Form), and the tassel holder is used to strike the opponent.

C.7

BRIEF:

Open your arms and squat.

DETAILS:

As you sink into a Half Sitting stance (or Cross-Sitting stance depending upon how low you wish to sink), separate your arms and open them, twisting the left palm so that it faces 6.00. The left hand points to 9.00, the sword running along the length of the outside of the left arm.

Your right hand moves downwards (palm up) to your right hip (as though wiping your waist with the back of the hand), and then continues out to your right side and back up to shoulder height with the fingers of the sword-hand pointing diagonally to 1.30 and parallel to the ground (still with palm up).

Your eyes look at your right hand.

57

NOTES:

- Avoid stepping too far ahead with the right foot; bend your knees so that you sink into the Half Sitting stance. To do this, turn your body to the right, and gently press the *outside* of the left thigh – just above the left knee – against the *outside* of your right calf (i.e. the knees will be crossed), and raise your left heel. Pressing the legs together will help your stability, as well as putting less strain on the knees. The weight will be fairly evenly ditributed over both feet.

- You can squat as low as you like in this move, but there is not a great deal to be gained by going too low.

- Keep the body upright.

- Ensure that you *arc* the right hand downwards and out to 1.30.

- A common mistake is to try to take the right arm too far behind you; it should point to 1.30, and not to 3.00, i.e. to your rear *diagonal*.

- The left arm must be rotated a quarter turn so that the sword lies between your arm and 6.00.

SECONDARY APPLICATION NOTES:

See comment above, but note that, in the posture, the head is turned away from the sword – which argues against the sword's use for an application.

However, I have seen this movement used against a thrust from behind, but in application, the squat is much lower, and the body leans over (to avoid the thrust), whilst the sword-fingers thrust to the heart of the opponent.

C.8

BRIEF:
Step with the left foot and start to arc the right hand towards the hilt.

DETAILS:
Leaving the left hand holding the sword in position, but turning the palm to face downward, move the weight completely on to the right foot and place the left heel to 9.00. Simultaneously the right sword-fingers arc upward past the right side of, and close to, the head (which starts to turn to 9.00, therefore the eyes initially follow the right hand).

NOTES:

- The width between the feet should be approximately 12 inches (30 centimetres).

C.9

BRIEF:
Move your weight forward and sword-fingers to the hilt of the sword.

DETAILS:
As your weight moves forward on to the left foot into a Bow stance, the body turns slightly to the left, and the right hand continues arcing up and then down to meet the left hand.

The sword-fingers of your right hand touch the hilt of the sword as the weight is fully transferred to the left foot. As your weight arrives on the left foot, slip your rear heel.

NOTES:

- Avoid lifting the right shoulder as your right hand sword-fingers touch the hilt.

- Be aware of the circular connection within the arms (possibly the third 'Halo').

The reason for this comparatively lengthy opening is that this is the traditional opening for the Yang Sword Forms.

Section 1

1 **Dragonfly Alights on the Water**
(Lit. Dragonfly skim water)

qīngtíng diǎnshuǐ

蜻蜓点水

Point Sword with Feet Together
(Lit. Feet Together – Diǎn)

bìngbù diǎnjiàn

并步点剑

APPLICATION:

点 = **diǎn** (*pron. "dee-en"*) dot; point; poke; jab; strike at a vital point.

A perpendicular sword where the tip of the sword is used to prod downwards as if pecking; the power passes to the tip of the blade.

Use the wrist to achieve this; the sword arm plays relatively little part in the stroke. The sword is mainly supported by the index and middle fingers; the other three fingers are relaxed. This connection of hand and sword therefore acts as a pivotal point so that the sword can move freely; it is important not to grip too tightly. This is not a large movement of the sword, but is usually quite a quick one. The purpose of **diǎn** is to attack an opponent's wrist, hand, or fingers of the arm that is holding the sword.

61

1.1

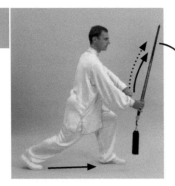

BRIEF:
Grasp the hilt and lower it as though 'drawing' the sword.

DETAILS:
The right hand grasps the hilt of the sword, and 'draws the sword', the hilt lowering so the blade is *starting* to become vertical. The weight is still on the left foot.

Open hand

Open hand reverse view

NOTES:

- The idea of 'drawing' the sword is only a visual idea to help achieve the correct movement. However, it has been suggested that up until this point the sword has been held by the left hand in a scabbard, and that one is now drawing it.

Grasp handle

1.2

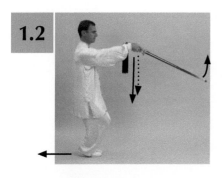

BRIEF:
Point the sword (**diǎn**).

DETAILS:
Only when the blade is vertical do you bring the right foot into the left foot. Simultaneously, the hand holding the hilt describes a small circle up and away from you as you push the tip of the sword in a larger arc away from you and slightly downwards, the tip of the blade dropping and pointing downwards by a maximum of 45°.

The tip of the blade therefore makes a large arc away and downwards whilst the hilt makes a smaller circle up and away only. The left sword-fingers touch your right wrist. The knees are both bent at the end of the movement. Both feet are together pointing to 9.00, with the heels flat on the floor, and the weight mainly on the left foot.

NOTES:

- When performing **diǎn**, the hilt always drops first toward the floor before rising up and away from your body. It is not unlike drawing a huge lower-case 'r' with the pommel, but note that the power in the downward stroke is in the hilt, but in the upward-and-away stroke is in the tip.

- In the final posture, your wrists are at the height of your shoulders.

- In the final posture, the tip of the sword is lower than your wrists; the arm and sword are not in a straight line therefore.

- A common mistake is to fail to relax the right shoulder. In order to keep the shoulder relaxed, it helps if you feel as though you are extending the right wrist *away* from you as you point the sword. So, although the energy should go to the tip of the sword, initially at least, try extending or pushing the wrist away from you.

- The feet should not be too close together in the final posture.

63

- The weight in the final posture should mainly be on the left foot, but keep the right foot flat.

- Keep the knees bent; avoid standing up too much.

PRIMARY APPLICATION NOTES:

This can be used as a strike to your opponent's hand that is holding his sword, or to his wrist. E.g. if your opponent thrusts his sword at you, side-step and use **diǎn**.

2	**Big Dipper** **(Lit. Big Chief Star Posture)**	**Stand on One Leg and Thrust** **(Lit. One-Legged Stance – Cì from Back)**
	dàkuí xīngshì	dúlì fǎncì
	大魁星势	独立反刺

APPLICATION:

刺 = **cì** *(pron. "tsir")* thrust; stab; prick; poke.

Thrusting the tip of the sword rapidly and powerfully straight at an opponent, the arm being extended from a bent position and making a straight line with the sword.

The power extends to the tip of the sword; if the blade-edges face left and right it is a flat thrust (***píng*cìjiàn**); if the blade-edges face up and down it is a perpendicular thrust (***lì*cìjiàn**). The thrust can be directed upward, downward, forward, backward, sideways, or overhead in an inverted thrust. The power of the thrust comes from the back leg combined with the turn of the waist. Once you have committed to this movement, it can leave you open to a counter-attack, should you miss your target.

> 撩 = **liāo** *(pron. "lee-ow" as in 'now')*
> lift up (e.g. a curtain); sprinkle; slide upward.
>
> Lifting upwards and away from the body with a perpendicular sword, the sword moving from behind you to ahead of you.
>   The power point is in the front part of the blade-edge; lift the tip of the blade upwards and forwards up an opponent's body. The blade can move from the left or right side of the body.

Tiǎo is not one of the 13 applications, but should be mentioned, as it appears at this point in the order of applications in the 32-Posture Sword Form.

挑 = **tiǎo** (*pron. "tee-ow" as in 'now'*) **carry on a pole.**

A vertical sword, letting the sword tip rise upwards like a carrying pole; the power is in the front part of the blade.

The tip of the sword thrusts at an opponent, possibly piercing the skin, and then cuts rapidly upward with a flick of the wrist. There is no arm movement; the entire action is performed by the flexion of the wrist.

2.1

BRIEF:
Step back with the right foot.

DETAILS:
First step back with your right foot to 1.30/2.00, leaving your weight on your left foot. Step with the ball of the right foot.

NOTES:

- This is a slightly widened step.

2.2

BRIEF:
As you move the weight on to the right foot, sweep the sword behind you to 1.30.

DETAILS:
Drop the hilt so that the tip of the blade lifts up slightly to approximately 45° (see APPLICATION NOTES below), and, as your weight moves over the right foot, lower the hilt so that it is in front of your abdomen, between your body and 12.00. Turn the body towards 12.00. The right foot should be placed so that the toes point to 11.00, i.e. the angle between left and right feet will be 60°.

The tip of the blade finishes slightly higher than the hilt.
The left sword-fingers follow the right wrist throughout.
The eyes follow the blade.

NOTES:

• The dropping of the hilt and the sitting back is the same feeling as pulling on a long rope in order to make the end of the rope jump towards you.

• Avoid dropping the head.

SECONDARY APPLICATION NOTES:
The initial lifting upward of the tip could be seen as cutting to an opponent's throat, under the chin.

The lowering of the blade is **chōu**: This can be seen as either an attack to the top of an opponent's wrist or arm, or even as a blocking down of his weapon.

Keep turning your body to 1.30, and pivot your left toes inwards to 12.00 (pivot on the heel). The lower edge of the blade cuts downwards past your right side, and then rises parallel to the ground to 1.30 with the lower edge of the blade now up, and the tip of the sword pointing to 1.30 (**liāo**). (N.B. This is not one of the 13 applications of the Form.) Your body will face 12.00 approximately.

Your left sword-fingers still point at the right wrist, palm down.

The eyes follow the tip of the sword.

NOTES:

- At this stage of the movement it is very tempting for beginners to turn the right foot. It is important not to move it.

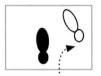

SECONDARY APPLICATION NOTES:

This could be cutting to the underside of an opponent's hand that is holding his sword, when he is standing at 1.30 (i.e. behind you, and to one side). To separate this as an application, if your opponent thrusts at you from behind, side-step, and then perform this move cutting to the underside of his hand. This would be using the movement like **liāo**.

68

2.3

BRIEF:
Rotate the blade.

DETAILS:
Without moving the tip, rotate the hilt so that the upper edge of the blade is now once again upwards (blade still parallel to the ground).

The left sword-fingers are still at the right wrist.

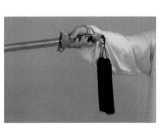

NOTES:

- This movement flows immediately into the following one.

2.4

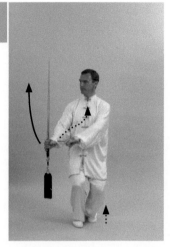

BRIEF:
Lift the tip of the sword.

DETAILS:
Draw the left foot into the right foot, in a T-step (toes touching the ground), and simultaneously the hilt lowers slightly to no lower than the waist, and the tip of the blade rises vertically.

The left sword-fingers draw back to the right elbow-crease, with palm still down.

The eyes look towards the tip of the sword.

NOTES:

- At this stage, the right foot has not moved, and is still pointing towards 11.00.

- The lifting of the tip of the sword is **tiāo** (see the APPLICATION notes at the start of Posture 2).

- The right hand during this action is initially at shoulder height, but then lowers slightly as the blade becomes vertical.

- The tip of the sword can be either vertical or angled slightly inwards towards your body.

2.5

BRIEF:
Lift the blade and stand on one leg.

DETAILS:
Stand up on the right foot raising the sword above your head and thrusting it to 9.00 and almost parallel to the ground (the tip should be slightly lower). The palm of your right hand therefore faces 12.00.

The left hand moves towards your centre (with fingers now lifting and palm facing to your right), and then arcs up via the chin (with palm turned away), before moving away to 9.00 with the fingertips vertical at eye height (and with the palm still turned away).

The left thigh is parallel to the ground with toes relaxed and pointing at the ground so that the sole of the foot faces your thigh, and the left knee points to 9.00.

The eyes look beyond the sword-fingers.

NOTES:

- The tip of the sword, the left sword-fingers, and the left knee are all in a vertical line, and the left sword-fingers are in line with the tip of the nose.

- The thigh being parallel to the ground is a *minimum* requirement. Leaving the knee pointing to 9.00, pull the sole of the left foot slightly to your right, therefore protecting the groin (but please note that this is also a stylistic point, rather than essential). The left knee and left elbow should be aligned.

- The right leg is straight, but not locked.

- Avoid holding the right hand too far away from your body, i.e. avoid pushing the sword towards 12.00.

- Relax your right shoulder; it is very easy to make the mistake of lifting it.

- This is taken from the original Yang Sword Form – 'The Big Dipper'. The application is **cì** (thrust), and its main purpose in the Posture is not because you are thrusting at anything in particular, but because it is demonstrating a balancing posture.

PRIMARY APPLICATION NOTES:
The application of this Posture is **cì**; therefore, there should be a feeling of the sword making an inverted thrust from back to front.

71

3	The Swallow Skims the Water (Lit. Swallow Flying Over the Water)	Sweep Sword in Crouch Step (Lit. Crouch Stance – Sideways Sǎo)
	yànzi chāoshuǐ	púbù héngsǎo
	燕子抄水	仆步横扫

APPLICATION:

扫 = **sǎo** (*pron. "sow" as in 'now'*) sweep.

A flat sword brandished and swung from left side to right side, or vice versa.

The arm and the sword make a straight line; the power is in the middle third of the blade-edge. The cut is often to the wrist or ankle. The height of **sǎo** is anywhere below the shoulders.

3.1

BRIEF:
Step back on the diagonal.

DETAILS:
Bend the right knee, and turn your body towards 1.30. As you do so, the blade of the sword cuts down to 1.30 as though doing **pī** (chop) with the right arm extended. (N.B. This is not one of the 13 applications of the Form.)

Simultaneously, lower your left foot to beside your right foot without placing any weight on it (and without touching the floor), and then move it to 7.30, stepping with the toes, and straightening the left knee. Your weight is still on the right foot. The left sword-fingers (palm down) touch the right wrist.

72

NOTES:

- This method of lowering the foot first, and *then* moving it backwards means that maximum control of balance is maintained.

- Avoid adjusting the right foot when stepping backwards.

- The sword and right arm should finish in a straight line.

- At the end of the move, the body still faces 1.30.

- Note that the textbook angle for the right foot is still pointing towards 11.00. However, some people prefer to turn the right foot to point towards 1.00 as it is more comfortable.

3.2

BRIEF:
Fingers to waist; sink into the right foot, lower the blade.

DETAILS:
The left hand leads off this movement by circling the *back* of the hand to your waist with the *fingers leading* (see part of the NOTES below). As the fingers reach the waist, sink into the right foot (forming a Crouching stance), and start to turn the body to 9.00 (to your left), sitting down and opening the Kua (see below). The right elbow drops toward the right knee and the left face of the blade turns upwards and parallel to the ground. Your eyes look at the tip of the sword.

The second photograph shows the same posture, but without sinking down so deeply. It can be performed either way.

Notes:

- It is not in the textbook that the fingers should lead, but it is usually performed in this way. Possibly this is taken from the threading hand movement in Bagua[1], but it is also more than likely that there is less chance of the left hand becoming trapped in the Kua, between the thigh and pelvis, when doing a low 'crouch step'. Either way is possible therefore, either left hand fingers leading, or the back of the left wrist, but the most common is to lead with the fingers in this particular move. (This also applies to the 42-Posture Sword Routine).

- Keep the right knee aligned with the right toes.

The Kua:

In the above case, this refers to the lateral rotation of the right thigh, or femur, in the pelvic socket. To be more accurate, the right thigh remains fixed, and it is the lateral or outward rotation of the *body* away from the thigh. In dance, or in ballet, this would be called 'turn out'. Anatomically this is the opening of the 'inguinal groove'.

74

3.3

Brief:
Pivot the left toes outward, transfer the weight on to the left foot, and adjust the right toes.

Details:
As you push your right foot into the floor, shifting your weight on to your left foot, pivot your left toes outward to 7.30. Move the weight over the left foot as you sweep the blade (still *parallel* to the ground) around to 9.00; adjust the right foot as you do so, pivoting on the *heel*. The sword finishes with the blade pointing at 9.00, on the

---

1   Bagua is a martial art based on the eight trigrams theory of the *Book of Changes (Yi Jing)*. □hile emphasising circular movements, the body is in a state of constant motion of which walking is the most important movement.

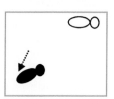

left side of your body (i.e. the hilt will be pointing at your left ribs), and the arm holding the sword well extended. The sword will finish at the height of your lower ribs.

Your left hand meanwhile circles out to 6.00 with the fingers leading, and then rises up above your head with the palm turned away.

The eyes look to 9.00.

NOTES:

- This is a diagonal Bow stance with the left foot pointing at 7.30.

- The method of turning the feet, as above, is important: Both feet pivot on the heel; turn the left toes first, and then turn the right toes.

- The movement of the blade in Posture 3 is (1) downward, then (2) horizontally, then (3) upward. Keep the sword lower than waist level, ideally at ankle or calf height.

- Make the Crouching stance as low as possible, and keep the left heel on the ground.

PRIMARY APPLICATION NOTES:
This could also be thought of as an attack to the legs of an opponent who is standing at approximately 11.00/12.00.

FURTHER PRIMARY APPLICATION:
Your opponent thrusts at you; sink into your right rear leg, i.e. into the move prior to the 'sweep' – his blade therefore passes over your back. Feed your left sword-fingers through the waist and then raise them to grasp the inside of his right wrist; whilst holding his right arm away, continue the 'sweep' movement attacking either his legs or waist with your sword.

4	Right Block and Sweep *(Has also been known as 'Swallow Moving Right')*	Horizontal Draw to the Right *(Lit. To the Right – Flat Dài)*
	yòu lánsăo	xiàngyoù píngdài
	右拦扫	向右平带

APPLICATION:

带 = **dài** *(pron. "dye")* belt; girdle; carry; bring; take back.

A flat sword drawn or whipped back from the front, to the side, and back; the power point is usually in the length of the blade-edge as a smooth movement, but it can also be in the tip (an attack to your opponent's wrist), or in the ridge of the blade (adhering to your opponent's blade). This is often thought of as 'carry back', as in 'draw back', or even 'slice back' (across the opponent's body), and involves the turn of the waist, and the flexing of the wrist. In other words, it is the full length of the blade-edge being drawn across your opponent's body or limb.

The movement is usually performed by extending the arm first, with the tip of the sword leading away from you, then rotating the body to left or right with the arm fairly well extended. Therefore keep the right elbow fairly open. (An analogy of this is to imagine a bicycle wheel lying on its side – the hub of the wheel is your centre. You extend the right arm (one of the spokes), and then rotate your centre so that the sword follows the outer movement of the rim (tyre) of the wheel.)

This is the horizontal equivalent of **chōu** (see below).

76

4.1

BRIEF:
Draw the sword and the foot in.

DETAILS:
Draw the right foot into the left foot (keeping the toes off the ground), and simultaneously draw the hilt of the sword back towards your left hip with the left face of the blade upwards. Lift the tip slightly, as you do so.

Your left sword-fingers (palm turning down) lower to touch your right wrist. The body turns to the left. The blade of the sword still points to 9.00.

The eyes look beyond the tip of the sword.

Alt. view

4.2

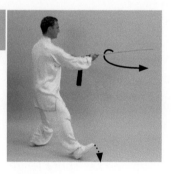

BRIEF:
Push the tip of the blade ahead and simultaneously place your right heel.

DETAILS:
Push the tip of the blade forwards to 9.00 (this can also be towards 8.00), with the right palm still up, and simultaneously place your right heel to 10.00 (30°) or to 10.30 (45°). The step is made together with the push of the blade.

The left sword-fingers move with the right wrist.

The eyes continue to look beyond the tip of the sword.

NOTES:

- The intention in this move is an extension of the arm to the corner, not a thrust (i.e. **cì**), although in effect this is what it is. Therefore don't perform it as a thrust, as it is only a transitional move. Its main function is to extend the right arm prior to the next movement.

BRIEF:
Turn the blade and cut across 9.00.

DETAILS:
Without moving the tip, your right palm turns downwards, so that the right face of the blade is now upwards, and, as you move your weight on to your right foot (which points at 10.00/10.30), turn your centre to your right and cut across on a 7.30/1.30 diagonal at chest height. The body now faces the right diagonal (10.00/10.30). Slip your left heel as necessary.

Your left sword-fingers still face the right wrist.
The eyes look to 9.00.

NOTES:

- This is a diagonal Bow stance with the right foot facing 10.00/10.30, but the opponent in the application is positioned at 9.00.

- The application of this move is **dài** (draw), and not **săo** (sweep). The feeling should be a cutting with the edge of the blade from front to back, or from well ahead of you on your left side, to nearer to you on your right side, as though running the entire length of the blade against an object in front of you. Avoid 'pushing' the blade away from you also. (See APPLICATION below.)

PRIMARY APPLICATION NOTES:
Awareness of the application helps: if you imagine that your opponent is standing facing you, between your body and 9.00. Push the tip of the blade to the left side of his body before stepping toward the right side of his body and drawing the edge of the blade across his chest or stomach, like a 'slice', from forwards-left and then backwards to your right.

5	Left Block and Sweep (Has also been known as 'Swallow Moving Left')	Horizontal Draw to the Left (Lit. Towards the Left – Flat Dài)
	zǔo lánsǎo	xiàngyoù píngdài
	左拦扫	向左平带

APPLICATION:

带 = **dài** (pron. "dye") belt; girdle; carry; bring; take back.

(See NOTES directly above.)

5.1

BRIEF:
Draw the left foot and the sword in.

DETAILS:
Draw the left (rear) foot into the right foot (keeping the toes off the ground), and simultaneously draw the hilt of the sword back towards your right hip with the right face of the blade upwards. Lift the tip slightly, as you do so. The blade of the sword now points to 9.00 again, and the body has turned to the right.

The eyes look beyond the tip of the sword.

NOTES:

• See 4.1 above.

79

5.2

BRIEF:
Push the tip of the blade ahead, step with your left foot to the corner, and sword-fingers to your waist.

DETAILS:
Push the blade forwards to 9.00 (this can also be towards 10.00), and simultaneously place the left heel to 8.00 (30°) or to 7.30 (45°). The step is made together with the push of the blade.

The left sword-hand starts to turn palm upwards and move back to the left hip with the wrist leading, the back of the wrist brushing the waist.

The eyes continue to look beyond the tip of the sword.

NOTES:

- See 4.2 above.

5.3

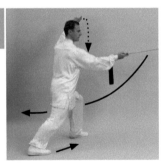

BRIEF:
Turn the sword and cut across 9.00.

DETAILS:
Without moving the tip, your right palm turns upwards, so that the left face of the blade is upwards, and, moving your weight on to your left foot (which points at 7.30/8.00), turn your centre to your left, and cut across on a 4.30/10.30 diagonal at chest height.

The back of your left sword-hand sweeps out to your left side, and then above your head, as you cut diagonally. The body now faces the left diagonal.

The eyes look to 9.00.

NOTES:

- This is a diagonal Bow stance with the left foot facing 7.30/8.00, but the opponent in the application is positioned at 9.00.

| **6** | **Searching In the Sea (Reaching Into the Sea Posture)**
 tànhǎi shì
 探海势 | **Stand on One Leg and Cut with Arm-Swing (Lit. One-Legged Stance – Circle and Pī)**
 dúlì lūnpī
 独立抡劈 |

APPLICATION:

劈 = **pī** (*pron. "peee"*) chop; hack; split open.

A perpendicular sword coming forcefully downwards from above. The power is in the middle section of the blade-edge, and, at the moment of contact in the chop, both arm and sword form a straight line. **Lūn pī** means to describe a big circle first and then chop. The movement can be initiated from high up on either your left or your right side. The chop finishes either parallel to the ground, or with the blade angled downward at 45°.

6.1

BRIEF:
Sweep the sword behind, and draw in your right foot.

DETAILS:
Draw the right foot into the left foot, touching the ground lightly with the toes. As you do so, the right hand sweeps down to your left side with the palm still upward, with the tip of the sword following. The sword moves diagonally downwards and then upwards towards 4.30 with the left *face* of the blade upward (i.e. your right palm is upward). The blade is almost, but not quite, parallel to the ground.

Alt. view

The left sword-fingers lower to above the right upper arm with the fingers pointing forwards and the palm down (the fingers are in front of the crease of the right armpit, and they can be extended further than this also – see below). The arms are therefore parallel to one another.

The eyes look at the tip of the sword at the end of the move.

NOTES:

- As the arm sweeps down to your left side, allow the wrist to flex, so that in effect, the tip is briefly left behind. As the arm moves upward behind you, straighten the wrist so that the tip lifts up behind you to 4.30. This avoids the tip of the sword touching the ground.

- When the arms are crossed, you can extend the left sword-fingers to *beyond* the outside of the right upper arm. Your left elbow will therefore be above the centre of the right forearm.

- Make sure that your body is turned towards 6.00.

6.2

BRIEF:
Turn hand and sword.

DETAILS:
Turn the sword so that the lower edge of the blade is upwards, i.e. your right palm faces away. Turn the left sword-fingers palm up.

The eyes still look at the tip.

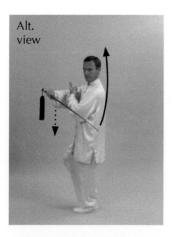

Alt. view

NOTES:

- This is a minor intermediate move, the left sword-fingers are still above the right arm, with the arms approximately parallel to each other, but both palms now face *away* from each other. In reality, this movement and the next happen together, but are easier to describe by splitting them. There is no harm in learning them separately, as they are then easier to combine.

6.3

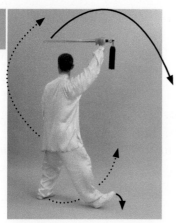

BRIEF:

Separate sword and hand (holding the ball), and step.

DETAILS:

Place the right heel to 9.00 as you raise the hilt of the sword above your head, but leave the tip 'hanging' downward behind you at 45°.

The left sword-fingers have dropped to Dantian height.

The eyes still look at the tip of the sword.

83

Alt. view

NOTES:

- Raise the hilt high because you are going to chop downwards.

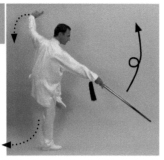

BRIEF:
Chop over; left knee raised.

DETAILS:
Move the weight on to your right foot and sweep the blade above your head and over to 9.00, until it points downward at 45°. Raise the left foot so the thigh is parallel to the ground, with the sole of the foot facing inwards toward the right thigh; your left knee points to 7.30/8.00.

The left sword-hand moves from palm up at the left side of the waist, out to the left side, and into the air above your head. At the end of the posture, the centreline of the body faces 7.30; the sword has chopped to 9.00, and the left hand is above your head in a circular shape from the fingertips to the hilt of the sword.

The body is angled forwards, and the eyes look at the tip of the sword.

NOTES:

- The supporting right foot will be turned slightly to the left (8.30) at the end of the move.

- In order to angle the body forward, bend from the pelvis, and avoid bending the back like a 'prawn'.

- A common mistake is to perform this movement as **diǎn**. Make sure that, at the end of the movement, the right shoulder and the tip of the sword are in a straight line; therefore avoid raising the wrist.

PRIMARY APPLICATION NOTES:
Chop straight down at opponent's head or shoulder.

7	Embrace the Moon *(Lit. Hugging the Moon to One's Bosom)*	Step Back and Withdraw Sword *(Lit. Backward Step – Chōu)*
	huáizhōng bàoyuè	tuìbù huíchōu
	怀中抱月	退步回抽

APPLICATION:

抽 = **chōu** (*pron. "cho" as in 'go'*) lash; whip; draw out; extract; pull; take out; draw along; draw back (like pulling a draw out of a chest of drawers, or drawing a letter from an envelope).

A perpendicular sword drawn or whipped back towards the body, with either an upward or a downward *arc*. The point of power is either in (approximately) the centre of the blade-edge, in the length of the blade-edge, or in the centre of the ridge depending upon whether the stroke is used for attack or for defence. For example, the edge of the blade, if placed under a limb, would be pulled back to make a cut, whereas the centre of the ridge of the blade could also be used to block a thrust.

This stroke is often thought of as 'draw back' or 'pull back' like **dài**, and the principles of **dài** apply to **chōu**; but in **chōu,** the sword blade is perpendicular. This stroke is not just used to attack; it also adopts the idea of neutralization.

In this Form, **chōu** appears three times, (Postures 7, 17, and 30), twice with an inverted perpendicular blade (Postures 7 and 30) in which the cutting or working edge of the sword is the upper one (an upward arc). In Posture 17, **chōu** occurs with the cutting or working edge of the blade being the lower one (a downward arc).

7.1

BRIEF:
Foot to the floor, and then foot back; turn the blade, then raise the sword.

DETAILS:
To step backward, first lower the left foot beside the right foot (without the toes touching the floor), and then, bending the right knee, move it behind you to 3.00, with the weight still on the right foot. As you do so, turn the lower edge of the blade upwards and, with the blade still angled downward at 30°–45°, raise it by about 2 feet (60 centimetres).

The left sword-fingers lower very slightly in the direction of the left side of your waist.

The eyes continue looking to 9.00.

NOTES:

- Step directly backward, but avoid making the stance too narrow. This is a slightly widened stance.

- As in 3.1, this method of lowering the foot first, and *then* moving it into Bow stance means that maximum balance control is maintained.

7.2

Alt. view

BRIEF:
Draw the sword up and back to your pelvis.

DETAILS:
As you move your weight back on to your left foot, arc the hilt of the sword upwards slightly and back down to the left side of your waist with the lower edge of the blade now upward at 45°. The distance of the hilt of the sword to your waist/hip is one to one and a half fist's distance. As your weight shifts back, lift your right toes, and then, drawing the right foot half a step, place the ball of the foot in an Empty stance.

The left sword-fingers move down to touch the pommel, or hilt, or the inside of the right wrist.

In the final posture, the centreline of your body faces 7.00/7.30; the right toes touch the ground in an Empty step. The sword is angled on a 4.00/10.00 axis, with the tip between your body and 9.00. The eyes look to 9.00 through the tip of the sword.

NOTES:

- When stepping back in move 1 with the left foot, step with an Empty left foot; avoid hurrying to move the weight backward.

- When moving into this posture, the hilt of the sword needs to *arc* from in front of you and back to your left side. Avoid drawing it back in a straight line.

- Sink deeply into the left foot, and relax.

- In the final posture, your right hand will be twisted inward to face your body; be careful not to grip the sword too tightly.

- Keep the elbows relaxed, and a slight space under the armpits.

- This has been described as 'putting the pommel of the sword into your waistcoat pocket'.

PRIMARY APPLICATION NOTES:

The sword during this movement is making a cut, e.g. under an arm, or to an opponent's hand or wrist. (E.g. If your opponent does **pī** (chop) to your head, you might side-step and lift the lower edge of your sword upwards under the hand with which he is holding his sword. You would then follow this with **cì** as Posture 8.)

The movement could also be seen as a purely defensive move – blocking the blade to the side.

8	**Evening Birds Returning to the Forest** *(Lit. Roosting Bird Flies Into the Forest)*	**Stand on One Leg and Thrust Upward** *(Lit. One-Legged Stance – Upward Cì)*
	sùniǎo tóulín	dúlì shàngcì
	宿鸟投林	独立上刺

APPLICATION:

刺 = **cì** (*pron. "tsir"*) thrust; stab; prick; poke.

Thrusting the tip of the sword rapidly and powerfully straight at an opponent, the arm being extended from a bent position and making a straight line with the sword.

The power extends to the tip of the sword; if the blade-edges face left and right it is a flat thrust (***píng**cìjiàn*); if the blade edges face up and down it is a perpendicular thrust (***lì**cìjiàn*). The thrust can be directed upward, downward, forward, backward, sideways, or overhead in an inverted thrust. The power of the thrust comes from the back leg combined with the turn of the waist. Once you have committed to this movement, it can leave you open to a counter-attack, should you miss your target.

8.1

BRIEF:
Turn the body to 9.00; sword to the centre of the body.

DETAILS:
Square your body to 9.00 as you move the hilt of the sword from the left hip to the centre of the body at waist height, with the left face of the blade facing upwards, and the sword still angled at 45°. (The tip of the blade still faces to 9.00.) As you do so, re-step to 9.00 with your right heel.

89

Alt. method

The left sword-fingers touch your right wrist.

The eyes look to 9.00.

NOTES:

- Alternatively, the hilt of the sword can also be brought to the right hip.

- When you re-step with the right heel, keep all the weight on the left foot.

8.2

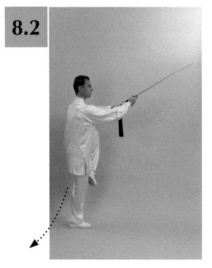

BRIEF:
Thrust upward on one leg.

DETAILS:
Move your weight on to your right foot, and thrust the sword upward in that direction, with the tip above your head. Raise the left foot so that the left thigh is parallel to the ground (see NOTES below).

The left sword-fingers stay on the right wrist (palm down), or can point at the pommel.

The tip of the sword is at the height of the top of your head.

The eyes look beyond the tip of the sword.

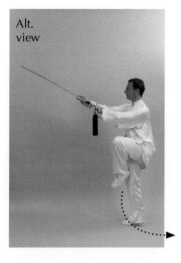

Alt. view

NOTES:

- Your hands should be at the same height as your shoulders.

- Your arms should be relaxed; avoid over-extending them.

- This is as though thrusting at an opponent's head, face, or neck.

- The left thigh is usually turned out to the left side slightly (30°), but with the left calf and sole of the foot pulled into the right leg. Point the left toes towards the floor.

- As in 2.3, the thigh being parallel to the ground is the *minimum* requirement.

PRIMARY APPLICATION NOTES:

Posture 7 followed by Posture 8 could be seen as a defensive move (7) followed by an offensive move (8). After the defence in 7 (above), re-step towards your opponent and thrust upward towards his throat.

Section 2

9	**Black Dragon Whipping its Tail** *(Lit. Black Dragon Swings its Tail)*	**Downward Intercept in Empty Stance** *(Lit. Empty Stance – Downward Jié)*
	wūlóng baĭweĭ	xūbù xiàjié
	乌龙摆尾	虚步下截

APPLICATION:

截 = **jié** (*pron. "jee-air"*) cut off (e.g. a length of something); intercept; block; separate into pieces (e.g. the concept of a dam across a river). You use the centre of the sword to 'divide' an object.

Cutting with a perpendicular sword or flat sword to parry and intercept the opponent. The power is in the blade-edge at the point of contact; if blocking another weapon, the bluntest third of the blade nearest the hilt, but it is better to use the sharper edge of the blade to block (cut) an opponent's sword arm or wrist, having evaded his attack. This should not be confused with **chōu** (in which the blade might be drawn backward as though 'slicing' using the length of the blade); this is a 'pressing' of the blade (e.g. downward).

APPLICATION NOTES:

Jié can be used downward, upward, forward, or from one side to the other. You can use **jié** downward on to an opponent's wrist, upward under an opponent's arm to attack his wrist, forward if he attacks using (e.g.) **dài**, or from the side:

E.g. Your opponent uses **pī** (chop) to your head; side-step to avoid the chop and then use **jié** to the side of his wrist using the centre of the blade with your sword vertical.

9.1

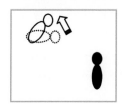

BRIEF:

Step left foot backward; sweep the sword across 6.00; slip the rear right heel.

DETAILS:

To step backward, first lower the left foot beside the right foot (without the toes touching the floor), and then, bending the right knee, move it behind you to 4.30, i.e. widen the stance as you step back.

NOTES:

- Step backward with the toes leading.

- As in 3.1, and 7.1, this method of lowering the foot first, and *then* moving it into the Side Bow stance means that maximum balance control is maintained.

Having placed your left foot, adjust your left heel so that the foot points to 6.00, and, transferring your weight over your left foot, turn the entire body to face 5.00/5.30. As you arrive in position, slip your right heel (i.e. pivot your right foot on the ball of the foot, so that the foot points at 7.30, the heel in constant contact with the floor – see 'Definitions of Terms Used'). You should be in a Side Bow stance.

Meanwhile the sword, left face up, cuts across the 6.00 direction towards your left, at throat height, with the blade parallel both to the ground and to the wall at 6.00, and with the tip pointing to 9.00.

The left sword-fingers move to the left hip with palm up.

NOTES:

- This is a Side Bow stance, so, whereas an ordinary Bow stance is greater in length than in width, a Side Bow stance is greater in width than in length.

93

- When stepping therefore, place the toes directly behind you to 3.00, but also slightly towards 6.00, thus slightly widening the stance when you eventually move into it. In the final posture, if you imagine a thick line of about 4 inches (10 centimetres) width, drawn from 9.00 to 3.00 between your feet, the heel of your right foot should be against one side of the line, and the toes of the left foot should be against the other side of the line. The toes of the left foot point to 6.00, and the toes of the right foot point to about 7.00/7.30.

- The distance between the feet (on a 12.00/6.00 axis) should be anywhere between 4–8 inches, or 10 to 20 centimetres.

- Problems that usually occur are (1) not widening the stance when stepping back with the left foot, (2) not keeping the blade parallel to the 6.00 wall, and (3) forgetting to slip the right heel.

SECONDARY APPLICATION NOTES:
This could also be a strike with the pommel of the sword to the left side.

BRIEF:
Turn the sword; sweep it to the right side; right toes to the corner.

DETAILS:
Keeping the weight on the left foot, start to turn your body back to your right, the tip of the sword sweeping around so that it now points to 3.00 instead of 9.00. (This is therefore a complete reversal of the sword.) The blade is then turned over so that the right face is upward (i.e. right hand palm down). Sweep the sword downward to outside your right thigh, so that it intercepts downward at approximately 45° with the lower edge of the blade, the tip of the sword facing 8.00.

As before, the left sword-fingers sweep from your hip, out to the left side, and then upward above your head.

As you sweep the sword down to your right side, the right toes move to 8.00 in an Empty stance, but there is a width between the feet of roughly 4 inches (10 centimetres).

The eyes look toward 10.30, i.e. over your right shoulder.

NOTES:

- This resembles 'Step Back to Repel Tiger' in the Yang Long Form, 3rd section.

- The turn of the sword at the end of 9.1 going into 9.2 (i.e. as you change the direction of the blade): avoid letting the blade waver from being parallel to the ground; there is a tendency for beginners to lift the tip of the sword upwards in order to turn the sword over.

95

- In the final posture, the width of the step avoids compressing the thighs together.

PRIMARY APPLICATION NOTES:

(1) The cutting edge of the perpendicular sword faces downwards by your side at the end of this posture as though someone is attacking with his sword from 9.00 10.30 and you are blocking downwards.

(2) The downward movement of the sword into the finishing posture could also be a downward attack (intercept) to the upper side of your opponent's wrist or arm.

(3) The movement of the right toes to 7.30 in an Empty stance could be thought of as though moving out of the way of a sword thrust or sweep.

COMBINED PRIMARY AND SECONDARY APPLICATION NOTES:

Stand in any neutral stance. As your opponent thrusts toward you, step back with your left foot, turning your body to your left, and 'slice' the sword to your left with the hilt leading (as in Posture 9.1 above); this is an attack to his right hand. Follow this with the movement as in Posture 9.2 above, cutting with your sword to your right side and attacking his leg(s). As your sword starts to move back to your right side, your left hand grasps his right hand, holding his sword away.

10 Green Dragon Emerges from the Water *(Green Dragon Coming Out of the Waves)*	Thrust in Left Bow Stance *(Lit. Left Bow Stance – Cì)*
qīnglóng chūshuǐ	zuǒ gōngbù cì
青龙出水	左弓步刺

APPLICATION:

刺 = **cì** *(pron. "tsir")* thrust; stab; prick; poke.

Thrusting the tip of the sword rapidly and powerfully straight at an opponent, the arm being extended from a bent position and making a straight line with the sword.

The power extends to the tip of the sword; if the blade-edges face left and right it is a flat thrust (*píng*cìjiàn); if the blade-edges face up and down it is a perpendicular thrust (*lì*cìjiàn). The thrust can be directed upward, downward, forward, backward, sideways, or overhead in an inverted thrust. The power of the thrust comes from the back leg combined with the turn of the waist. Once you have committed to this movement, it can leave you open to a counter-attack, should you miss your target.

97

10.1

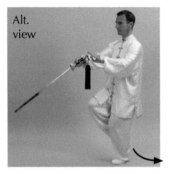

Alt.
view

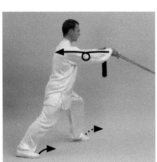

BRIEF:
Lift hilt; lift right foot, and place it behind you.

DETAILS:
Draw the right foot beside the left foot and, extending the sword away from you towards 8.00, raise it (the lower edge of the blade still facing down), with the tip angled slightly down (30°), and the right wrist relaxed.

The left sword-fingers lower to touch the right wrist.

As the sword arrives in the above position, place the right toes behind you to 1.30, keeping the weight on the left foot.

The eyes look at the tip of the sword.

NOTES:

- This should not be thought of as either **diǎn** (point) or **cì** (thrust) to 8.00.

- The wrist is higher than the tip of the sword as you step back with the right foot.

- Some people prefer not to let the tip drop on lifting it, but to keep it parallel to the ground.

SECONDARY APPLICATION NOTES:
Potentially another attack to the underside of an opponent's wrist.

10.2

BRIEF:
Draw the hilt back; turn the body; slip the left heel.

DETAILS:
As you move your weight over your right foot, pivot the foot on the ball so that the toes then point towards 10.30/11.00, turning your body so that your centreline moves towards 10.30. Simultaneously, gently *arc* the sword backward with the turn of the body, turning the hilt of the sword so that the lower edge of the blade turns upwards, and drawing it back to between eye and mouth height (your right palm will now face away from you). The tip still points to 8.00 (i.e. the direction in which you are about to thrust the sword). As you complete the turn, slip the left heel.

The left sword-fingers follow the right wrist.

The eyes look over your left shoulder at the tip of the sword.

NOTES:

- The 'arc' of the sword should only be a slight one.

- The centre of the blade will be in front of your face.

- The sword will be approximately parallel to the ground, although the tip might be slightly dropped.

- Be careful not to alter the angle of the blade (i.e. on the 8.00/2.00 axis) as you draw it back.

SECONDARY APPLICATION NOTES:
This could be a cut under the opponent's wrist or arm, or possibly even a strike with the tassel holder to 1.30.

10.3

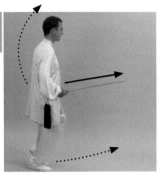

BRIEF:
Turn to 8.00; both palms turned up by the hips.

DETAILS:
Draw the left foot in towards the right foot, turning the body to face 8.00. As you do so, lower the hilt of the sword to beside your right hip, turning your right palm up.

Simultaneously, draw your left sword-fingers (also with palm up) to the front of your abdomen.

The eyes look to 8.00.

NOTES:

- When drawing in the left foot, the toes should not touch the ground.

- When lowering the sword, avoid drawing it backwards any further, just lower the blade vertically in an arc that goes outward and then inward to the waist.

10.4

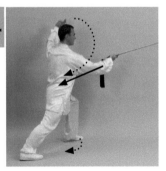

BRIEF:
Step to 8.00 and thrust.

DETAILS:
Place your left heel to 8.00, and move the weight over the left foot into a Bow stance as you thrust in that direction with the left face of the blade upward. The tip thrusts to chest (heart) height.

Meanwhile the left sword-fingers circle from the left side of your waist, out to your left side, and then up above your head.

NOTES:

- Keep a width of 12 inches (30 centimetres) between the feet in this posture.

PRIMARY AND SECONDARY APPLICATION NOTES:

When your opponent thrusts his sword at you, step to your right to avoid the thrust, then lift your sword (which blocks his sword upward, or attacks the underside of his wrist) as in Posture 10.1. As you step behind and sit back onto your right foot, turn your sword (thus either keeping his sword away from you, or cutting his wrist/fingers holding his sword) as in Posture 10.2. Then, as in Posture 10.4, follow with **cì** (thrust). Your left hand blocks/lifts his right hand (holding his sword) upward.

11	The Wind Blowing on the Lotus Leaves (Lit. Wind Curls the Lotus Leaves)	Turn Around and Draw Slanting Sword (Lit. Turn Body – Oblique Dài)
	fēngjuǎn héyè	zhuǎnshēn xiédài
	风卷荷叶	转身斜带

APPLICATION:

带 = **dài** (*pron. "dye"*) belt; girdle; carry; bring; take back.

A flat sword drawn or whipped back from the front, to the side, and back.

The power point is usually in the length of the blade-edge as a smooth movement, but it can also be in the tip (an attack to your opponent's wrist), or in the ridge of the blade (adhering to your opponent's blade). This is often thought of as 'carry back', as in 'draw back', or even 'slice back' (across the opponent's body), and involves the turn of the waist, and the flexing of the wrist.

11.1

BRIEF:
Sit back, pivot the left foot, and 'cover' the sword.

DETAILS:
Sit back on to the right foot and pivot the left foot on the heel so the toes point to a minimum of 10.30 (the further round you are able to turn them, the easier the following move is).

Simultaneously, bend your elbow, and draw the sword back (still left face of the blade up) in front of the chest/solar plexus (with the right arm bent).

Lower your left sword-fingers (with palm down) to touch your right wrist. The left elbow is well opened and is *roughly* in line with the blade, as though the forearm is 'covering' it. The body faces approximately 10.30.

NOTES:

- Do not open the left elbow too far.

11.2

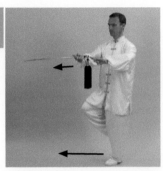

BRIEF:
Sit back again; extend the sword; place your right foot.

DETAILS:
Shift the weight completely on to the left foot (see NOTES on p.104, for a method of making this move easier) raising the right thigh, and keep turning the body clockwise to your right, towards 3.00.

NOTES:

- When raising the right thigh, avoid lifting it too high; keep the sole of the right foot opposite the calf.

Push with the tip of the sword to 1.00/1.30 (the blade at about chest height, and the left face of the sword still upwards), i.e. extend the radius of the part-circle you are about to create. (This is the push of the sword to the 'corner' before **dài**: see NOTES below.)

The left sword-fingers still touch your right wrist.

NOTES:

- I have seen the 'push with the tip of the sword' done to a variety of different directions – anywhere between 10.30 and 1.30. (My personal preference is to push the sword out to about 1.00.) The most important thing is that the sword *is* pushed out before being drawn back, i.e. it has to go out, before circling around to the right; how early one does it is probably academic. In order to perform **dài**, the sword must be pushed in the opposite direction first, thereby extending the arm/elbow and the radius of the horizontal arc that you are about to create in the following movement.

- N.B. This is only an extension of the sword to the side or corner; it is not a 'thrust' (**cì**).

BRIEF:
Place right foot and turn sword, Bow stance, and **dài**.

DETAILS:
Place your right heel to 4.00, and as you move your weight on to your right foot, turn the sword over so that the right face of the blade is now uppermost. Then, cut diagonally on a 1.30/7.30 axis; your opponent would be standing at 3.00. Adjust the left foot by slipping the heel. The blade is at chest height, with the blade angled upward very slightly.

    The left sword-fingers (with palm down) follow the right wrist.

    The eyes look to 3.00.

NOTES:

- Make sure that you place the *heel*, and not the toes, at 4.00.

- This is a *narrow* Bow stance approximately 4 inches (10 centimetres) wide.

- When turning toward 3.00, allow the pelvis to open wide, and avoid the left knee collapsing inwards.

- This entire Posture involves a turn of the body of 240°.

- There is a method of making this turn much easier. In its present form, the last part of this movement requires an opening of the pelvis of at least 120°, depending upon how far you are able to turn your left toes at the end of 11.1. In order to lessen the amount of turn-out necessary: Having sat on to the right foot and turned your left toes in 11.1, as you are starting to sit back again on to the left foot in 11.2, pivot your left heel outwards (clockwise) as far as you are able, and then continue to place your weight fully on to it.

PRIMARY APPLICATION NOTES:

With all the **dài** applications, the principle is similar. There is always a 'push' with the tip of the sword to the corner, and then the blade is drawn from one side to the other. In effect what you are doing is 'pushing' the blade to one side of an opponent's body, e.g. in the above example to the left of his body, before drawing the edge of the blade across to the other side of his body, to make a 'slicing' action.

| **12** The Lion Shakes its Head (Lit. Lion Nods its Head)

shīzi yáotoú

狮子摇头 | **Retreat and Carry Slanting Sword** *(Lit. Recoil Body – Oblique Dài)*

suō hēn xiédài

缩身斜带 |

APPLICATION:

带 = **dài** *(pron. "dye")* belt; girdle; carry; bring; take back.

(See NOTES directly above.)

12.1

Alt. view

BRIEF:
Bring the sword and foot in.

DETAILS:
Without turning the sword over (i.e. the right face is still uppermost), draw the hilt back towards the right hip allowing the tip to move towards 3.00/4.00. Simultaneously, draw your left foot into the right foot with the toes not touching the ground.

Your left sword-fingers start to move backward towards your waist.

106

BRIEF:
Push the sword to the corner; thread left sword-fingers; step back.

DETAILS:
Still without turning the sword, push the tip of the sword to 4.00, and, with the weight still on your right foot, place your left foot in the same position as at the end of Posture 11. Simultaneously, your left wrist folds inwards, and your left sword-fingers lead (with palm up) to the left side of your waist (i.e. the back of your hand rubbing your waist) to thread behind you. You extend the left arm so that the fingers point to 10.00/10.30, the palm still twisted upwards.

NOTES:

- This is the only time in the Form that it is a requirement that the fingers lead the wiping of the waist.

- The toes of the right foot should be pointing to 4.00 still, and therefore the sword should be sent out in the same direction.

BRIEF:
Turn the sword over, and draw it back transferring your weight.

DETAILS:
As you sit back on to the left foot, turn your right palm up (left face of the blade turning upwards), and draw your right foot back into a T-stance (with toes touching the ground). Draw the hilt of the sword back with the tip slightly raised, to finish opposite your chest on the 4.00/10.00 axis.

Your left sword-fingers (with palm down) arc forwards to touch your right wrist.

Your centreline now faces 1.30.

Your eyes look towards the tip of the sword.

NOTES:

- The arms/elbows are partially extended.

- This is the first T-stance in the routine.

- Note that this is not an Empty stance.

PRIMARY APPLICATION NOTES:

As you thrust the sword forward and then pull it backwards to the left side of the body, it is cutting across the side of the chest or the arm from front to back. (See **dài** above).

13	Tiger Covers its Head *(Lit. Tiger Holds its Head)*	Raise Knee and Hold Sword with Both Hands *(Lit. Raise Knee – Pĕng)*
	hŭbàotóu	tíxī pĕngjiàn
	虎抱头	提膝捧劍

Pĕng is not one of the 13 applications, but should be mentioned as it appears at this point in the order of applications in the Form. Posture 13 also takes its name from it.

捧 = **pĕng** *(pron. "pung" as in 'lung')* hold/offer with both hands.

Supporting a perpendicular or flat sword with both hands in front of the body as if making an offering; same as **bào** (抱) but **pĕng** is usual.

13.1

BRIEF:
Push, sit back, and separate hands.

DETAILS:
Still looking towards the tip of the sword, push the blade to 2.00 (palm up/left face up), and place your right foot to 8.00 behind you (i.e. as in a widened Bow stance).

Turn the sword over (palm down/right face up), and, sitting back on to your right foot, draw the hilt of the sword to your right side.

Alt. view

Alt. view

Your left sword-fingers follow the right wrist. When the hilt reaches your right side, open your arms so that the sword finishes diagonally on the 1.30/7.30 axis, with the tip slightly raised. The left hand mirrors the position of the right hand.

The sword should be almost parallel to the ground (the tip is slightly raised). The tip of the sword is directly between the centreline of your body and 3.00.

Your left toes move into the centreline as you complete the movement (with the separation of the arms).

The eyes look straight ahead.

NOTES:

- Sometimes the action of the left sword-fingers is done slightly differently; the left hand follows the right wrist for part of the way, but the arms are separated halfway back.

- In the final posture, the arms are not pulled backwards behind the line of the shoulders, but form a gentle arc, so that the left hand (if it were holding another sword) would be touching the tip of the first sword. In other words, the elbows on either side are slightly forward of the body rather than being level with the body.

SECONDARY APPLICATION NOTES:

This second cut also cuts across your opponent's side, chest, or arm.

The sitting back and slicing from left to right is **dài** again.

13.2

BRIEF:
Re-step, open the arms, then swing arms and sword inward, lifting the knee.

DETAILS:
Step a half pace forward (toward 3.00) with the left heel, lifting both the left hand and sword to chest height (but still below shoulder level). The tip of the sword still points ahead to 3.00. Move the weight on to your left foot, and then, turning the left face of the blade upward (palm up), move the hilt into your centreline with the blade at chest height, parallel to the ground, and still pointing to 3.00.

    The left sword-fingers mirror the action of the right hand, moving outward, and then inward to finish (palm up) under the right hand. (See NOTES below.) As the hands come together, extend the arms ahead of you, but leave the arms relaxed and slightly bent.

NOTES:

- This movement is sometimes seen performed slightly differently. The tip of the sword is *swung* out to your right so that it briefly points to 4.30 or beyond, and then *swung* back inwards ahead of you; therefore, in effect, the blade makes a sideways 'chop'. This strictly speaking is incorrect, as the meaning of the word **pěng** (捧) is to 'offer' the blade.

- The left hand is sometimes held as though 'cupping' the right hand, i.e. with an open palm under the back of the right hand. This is also known as 'Holding the Tiger's Head'.

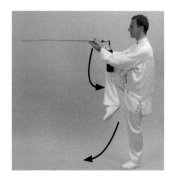

Simultaneously, stand up on the left foot (the leg is straight), drawing the right foot in, and raising the knee in front of you with your thigh parallel to the ground (this is the minimum height). The sole of the right foot should face the left thigh, and the right knee should point straight ahead.

At the end of the movement, the tip of the blade is at the height of the upper chest, the blade is angled very slightly upward.

NOTES:

• 'Artistically' the right knee, instead of being lifted straight up, can be 'spiralled' outward and upward to the right side, and then back into the centre again.

PRIMARY APPLICATION NOTES:

Pěng has no real martial meaning, and this Posture can be looked on as preparation for the following Posture. However, I have seen '**pěng**' being used in application to lift up an opponent's sword as he does **cì**, almost 'flicking' it up, prior to thrusting.

14 Wild Horse Jumps Over the Ravine
(Lit. Wild Horse Jumps the Mountain Stream)

yěmǎ tiàojiàn

野马跳涧

Jump Step and Flat Thrust
(Lit. Jump Step – Flat Cì)

tiàobù píngcì

跳步平刺

APPLICATION:

刺 = **cì** (*pron. "tsir"*) thrust; stab; prick; poke.

Thrusting the tip of the sword rapidly and powerfully straight at an opponent, the arm being extended from a bent position and making a straight line with the sword.

The power extends to the tip of the sword; if the blade-edges face left and right it is a flat thrust (*píng*cìjiàn); if the blade-edges face up and down it is a perpendicular thrust (*lì*cìjiàn). The thrust can be directed upward, downward, forward, backward, sideways, or overhead in an inverted thrust. The power of the thrust comes from the back leg combined with the turn of the waist. Once you have committed to this movement, it can leave you open to a counter-attack, should you miss your target.

14.1

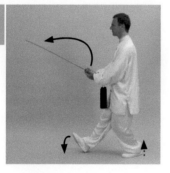

BRIEF:
Sink and drop the hilt, drawing it slightly backward.

DETAILS:
Bend the leg you are standing on slightly and, as you place your right heel ahead of you to 3.00, lower the hilt of the sword slightly, and draw it back towards your body, leaving the tip approximately at the same height. (The hilt should go no lower than waist height.)

NOTES:

- Keep the weight on the left foot.
- Keep the body upright.

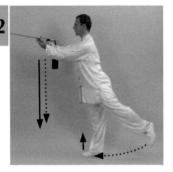

BRIEF:
Weight forward, and push the tip forward, lifting the hilt.

DETAILS:
As you transfer your weight on to your right foot, raise the hilt to chest height (the tip of the blade now only slightly raised). As the hilt rises, extend your arms ahead of you, but leave the left toes touching the floor as though they have been left behind. (This movement is almost balletic in style; the weight should almost *tip* forward in slow motion, with the left leg remaining extended behind.)

Your left sword-fingers are palm up under your right wrist throughout.

NOTES:

- This is really a 'jump' in order to gain ground for the **cì** that follows, but in this Form it is not performed as such. In the traditional Yang Sword Forms, there is an actual leap.

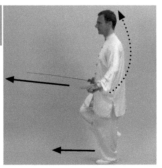

BRIEF:
Fall on to the left foot; 'drop' the hilt and sword-fingers.

DETAILS:
As your weight tips forward, step through with your left foot (i.e. ahead of your right foot), literally 'falling' (gently) on to it, and, as you land on it, draw your right foot into your left calf, with the foot off the ground at ankle height. The toes of the left foot should be turned out slightly.

Simultaneously, rapidly push your palms downward to hip height, separating them to either side of you. Keep the tip of the sword slightly raised. Both your left and right palms are turned down.

NOTES:

- When 'jumping', there is a brief moment when both feet are off the ground.

- When landing from the jump on the left foot, make sure that you cushion the landing by bending the left knee.

- This can be rather an abrupt movement, and should be performed as smoothly and lightly as possible. The landing on the left foot, the hands pressing rapidly to waist height (approximately), and the right foot drawing into the left foot should all be simultaneous.

- If using the 'open left hand' position, the pushing down of the sword and left hand (i.e. the end of the jump) is the moment when you re-form the sword-fingers.

- Do not pause when you land on to the left foot, move straight into the thrust that follows.

SECONDARY APPLICATION NOTES:
There is no application as such for this pushing down of the hand and sword, but I have come across its being described as **Yā** (压), where the blade pushes down on an opponent's weapon with the face of the blade, prior to thrusting.

115

14.4

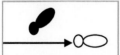

BRIEF:
Step and thrust.

DETAILS:
As you place the right heel to 3.00, turn the left face of the blade up, drawing the hilt into the right side of your waist.

Transfer your weight on to your right foot and drive the tip of the sword directly forwards to 3.00 at chest height, with the blade parallel to the ground, and with the left face of the blade still up.

The left sword-fingers circle outward to your left side, and then upwards to above your head.

NOTES:

- The width of this stance is about 4 inches (10 centimetres).

15 Little Dipper (Lit. Little Chief Star Posture)

xiǎokuíxīng shì

小魁星势

Circle Sword in Left Empty Stance (Lit. Left Empty Stance – Liāo)

zuǒ xūbù liāo

左虚步撩

APPLICATION:

撩 = **liāo** (*pron. "lee-ow" as in 'now'*) lift up (e.g. a curtain); sprinkle; slide upward.

Lifting upwards and away from the body with a perpendicular sword, the sword moving from behind you to ahead of you.

The power point is in the front part of the blade-edge; lift the tip of the blade upwards and forwards up an opponent's body. The blade can move from the left or right side of the body.

15.1

BRIEF:
Sit back and circle the sword to your left side.

DETAILS:
As you sit back facing 1.30, turn the lower edge of the blade upwards, raise the hilt of the sword, and draw it back in an anticlockwise arc, rising up and back, and then down to the left side of your waist, with the blade pointing upward at 45° to 11.00. Draw the right foot back into the left foot, with toes touching the ground.

The centreline of your body will face 12.00 approximately.

NOTES:

- This is the first circular cut.

- There is a feel of leaving the tip of the sword behind whilst arcing over.

- Keep the sword close to the body.

The left sword-fingers lower to touch the right wrist.

The eyes look at the tip of the sword, i.e. towards 10.30/11.00.

SECONDARY APPLICATION NOTES:
This could potentially be either a deflection of an opponent's sword, or even an attack – cutting (e.g.) under an opponent's arm or wrist.

 15.2

BRIEF:
The sword circles downward and place the heel.

DETAILS:
As you start to turn your body to the right, place your right heel to 3.00, and simultaneously the blade continues to circle down, so that it is almost parallel to the ground.

The left sword-fingers continue to follow the right wrist.

The eyes still look toward the tip of the sword.

NOTES:

- The movements of the right foot stepping out and the sword cutting down are simultaneous.

15.3

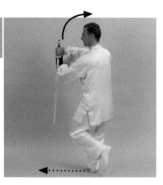

BRIEF:
Weight forward on to the right foot; circle the sword up on your right; left toes in an Empty step.

DETAILS:
As you transfer your weight over your right foot, turn your right toes outward to 45° (i.e. to point to 4.30). As you turn your body to 4.30, sweep the tip of the sword from your left side, up ahead of you, so that the underside of the tip of the blade cuts up in front of you.

The end of the movement is with the hilt slightly above head height, with the hilt opposite (and above) the right side of the head, and the blade angled slightly downward.

The left sword-fingers (which have followed your right wrist throughout) still point at your right wrist, although sometimes they are lowered slightly to touch the right forearm.

Your weight is on your right foot and the toes of the left foot touch the ground ahead of you in an Empty step.

Your eyes look to 3.00.

NOTES:

• It is the *tip* of the sword that is doing the work; so ensure that the tip is only dropped very slightly at the end of the posture.

• The blade will be angled slightly downward at the end of the move.

PRIMARY APPLICATION NOTES:
The application for moves 1, 2, and 3 above are: Your opponent thrusts toward you, from 3.00. Sit back, brushing the opponent's sword to your left, and continue to circle your sword, the tip moving downward and then back up between your opponent's legs.

16 Scooping the Moon from the Bottom of the Sea
(Lit. Dredge Seabed for Moon)

Seahaǐdǐ lāoyuè

海底捞月

Circle Sword in Right Bow Stance
(Lit. Right Bow Stance – Liāo)

yòu gōngbù liāo

右弓步撩

APPLICATION:

撩 = **liāo** (*pron. "lee-ow" as in 'now'*) lift up (e.g. a curtain); sprinkle; slide upward (see Posture 15).

16.1

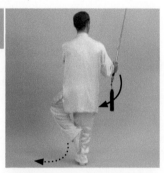

Alt. view

BRIEF:
Circle the sword behind you on your right side.

DETAILS:
As you turn your centreline to face 6.00, circle the tip of the sword upward and outward to 7.30 to finish with the hilt down by your right hip, and with the blade angled upward at 45°. Draw the left foot into the right ankle.

The left sword-fingers follow the right wrist.

The eyes follow the tip of the blade.

NOTES:

• Some practitioners leave the left foot ahead without moving it.

119

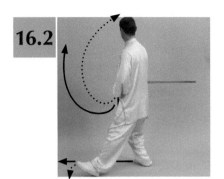

16.2

BRIEF:
The sword circles downward, re-step with the left heel, weight forwards on to the left foot.

DETAILS:
Step to 3.00 with the left foot again, turning it out at 45°, and, as you cut down with the lower edge of the blade to your right side, start to move your weight forward over the left foot.

Your left sword-fingers start to move to your waist (palm up).

Alt.
view

NOTES:

• At this stage, the sword is on your right side, with the blade almost parallel to the ground.

16.3

BRIEF:
Transfer the weight and sweep the blade up ahead of you.

DETAILS:
Transfer your weight fully on to your left foot, and immediately step through to 3.00 with the right foot into a right Bow stance. Simultaneously, the lower edge of the blade rises to finish facing 3.00. The sword is well extended away from you, with the tip slightly lowered, and your right hand at about the height of your right shoulder.

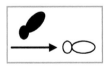

Your left sword-fingers extend out to your left side, and then rise above your head.

Your eyes look toward 3.00.

NOTES:

- This is a narrow Bow stance with a width of approximately 4 inches (10 centimetres).

- The right sword arm and right leg move together on the step through.

- Finish with the blade either parallel or almost parallel to the ground.

PRIMARY APPLICATION NOTES:

This is as though slicing up the centreline of an opponent's body. (See APPLICATION NOTES on p.117.)

Section 3

17	**Shooting at the Wild Geese** ***(Lit. Shooting Geese*** ***Posture)*** shèyàn shì 射雁势	**Turn Around and** **Withdraw Sword** ***(Lit. Twist Body – Chōu)*** zhuǎnshēn huíchōu 转身回抽

APPLICATION:

抽 = **chōu** (*pron. "cho" as in 'go'*) lash; whip; draw out; extract; pull; take out; draw along; draw back (like pulling a draw out of a chest of drawers, or drawing a letter from an envelope).

A perpendicular sword drawn or whipped back towards the body, with either an upward or a downward *arc*. The point of power is either in (approximately) the centre of the blade-edge, in the length of the blade-edge, or in the centre of the ridge depending upon whether the stroke is used for attack or for defence. For example, the edge of the blade, if placed under a limb, would be pulled back to make a cut, whereas the centre of the ridge of the blade could also be used to block a thrust.

This stroke is often thought of as 'draw back' or 'pull back' like **dài**, and the principles of **dài** apply to **chōu**; but in **chōu**, the sword blade is perpendicular. This stroke is not just used to attack; it also adopts the idea of neutralization.

In this Form, **chōu** appears three times, (Postures 7, 17, and 30), twice with an inverted perpendicular blade (Postures 7 and 30) in which the cutting or working edge of the sword is the upper one (an upward arc). In Posture 17, **chōu** occurs with the cutting or working edge of the blade being the lower one (a downward arc).

This Posture is made up of two Postures from the Traditional Yang Tàijí Sword, 'The Rhino Looking at the Moon', and 'Shooting the Wild Goose'.

17.1

BRIEF:
Sit back; then turn the body.

DETAILS:
First, start to sit back on to the left foot, still facing 3.00.

Then, as you turn your body toward 12.00, turn your right toes pivoting on the heel, and simultaneously draw the sword back at throat height, with the lower edge of the blade still uppermost and parallel to the ground. The blade is approximately on the 10.30/4.30 diagonal, and is between your body and 12.00.

Your left sword-fingers lower to touch your right wrist.
The eyes still look at the tip of the blade.

NOTE:

- Keep the left elbow well open, so that the left forearm is not far from being parallel to the ground, the elbow pointing to your right.

17.2

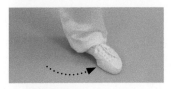

BRIEF:
The blade 'chops' to 10.30/11.00; adjust the left foot.

DETAILS:
With the weight remaining on your left foot, the sword then cuts up and over (chops over) to 10.30/11.00, so that the blade finishes parallel to the ground. As it does so, there is a left foot adjustment – turn your left toes outwards whilst the weight is on that foot, pivoting on the heel so that the toes face 10.30.

The left sword-fingers follow the right wrist.

SECONDARY APPLICATION NOTES:
This is **pī** (chop), but is not one of the 13 main applications. Allow the right elbow to fully open as you chop.

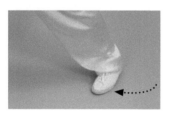

BRIEF:
Lift the tip of the sword, and immediately sweep the blade downward and back, moving the weight back on to the right foot.

DETAILS:
From this position, there is a slight upward 'flick' or 'lift' with the tip of the sword followed by a drop of the hilt, and, as you sit back on to the right foot and turn the body toward 12.00, the lower edge of the blade cuts downward past, and close to, your right side. The hand holding the sword moves down past your right thigh, and then slightly back up again as it passes your body; the *arm* points to 1.30, but the blade of the sword is pointing downward at about 45°.

As you sit back on to the right foot and turn the centre to 12.00, you can pivot the toes of the left foot so that they turn towards 1.30; this is not essential, but helps the lifting in of the foot in the move to come.

The left sword-hand follows the right wrist throughout.

The eyes look toward the right wrist.

NOTES:
- Relax your left elbow, and make sure that the body is turned to the right.

- The feel of this part of the movement is a little like flicking a rope back towards you when you are holding one end. You lift the end that you are holding (the hilt) and then drop it again in order to create a reaction at the end of the rope (the tip).

124

17.4

BRIEF:
Left sword-fingers to the corner.

DETAILS:
Turn your body back to 10.30 and simultaneously bring your left sword-fingers in towards your centre (heart height, with fingers now vertical and palm turning away), up to your chin (fingers still vertical), and circle them, from your chin, out ahead of you to 10.30. As your left sword-fingers arrive in position, with fingers vertical and palm facing away from you, place the toes of your left foot ahead of you in an Empty stance to 10.30.

Simultaneously, pull the pommel of the sword slightly backwards to 4.00, but not so far that your elbow moves behind the line of your back. At the end of the move, the tip of the sword is angled downwards. The body is turned towards 10.30.

The eyes look to 10.30, beyond the left sword-fingers.

NOTES:

- Ensure that the sword creates a straight line from the start of its downward cut to the end of it. In other words, the line drawn by the pommel from 10.30 to 4.30 should be straight; don't try to lift the blade sideways and away from the body.

- Make sure that the pommel of the sword is pulled slightly back behind your right hip, but because of the turn of the body, you should not be pulling it behind your back.

- Be careful that you don't allow the right knee to collapse inward.

- In the final posture, eyes, toes, and left sword-fingers are all pointing in the same direction. The blade, although pointing downward, is also pointing in the same direction.

PRIMARY APPLICATION NOTES:
The application of this Posture is not the final move, but is the action of the sword cutting back and down from 10.30/11.00. This is **chōu**. This is like a 'slash' that moves downward, possibly to a leg, or to the hand or wrist of an opponent's arm, but it could also be a defensive stroke.

18	**White Ape Offers Fruit** *(Lit. White Ape Offers Up Fruit)*	**Thrust Flat Sword with Feet Together,** *(Lit. Feet Together – Flat Cì)*
	baíyuán xiànguǒ	bìngbù píngcì
	白猿献果	并步平刺

APPLICATION:

刺 = **cì** *(pron. "tsir")* thrust; stab; prick; poke.

Thrusting the tip of the sword rapidly and powerfully straight at an opponent, the arm being extended from a bent position and making a straight line with the sword.

The power extends to the tip of the sword; if the blade-edges face left and right it is a flat thrust (***píng*cìjiàn**); if the blade-edges face up and down it is a perpendicular thrust (***lì*cìjiàn**). The thrust can be directed upward, downward, forward, backward, sideways, or overhead in an inverted thrust. The power of the thrust comes from the back leg combined with the turn of the waist. Once you have committed to this movement, it can leave you open to a counter-attack, should you miss your target.

BRIEF:
Left foot in, and then out to 9.00; 'balance' the arms.

DETAILS:
Turn the body towards 9.00. As you do so, allow the left hand, leading with the heel of the hand, to move to your left with the turn of the centre, the palm still facing away from you. Your right hand starts to move inwards and upwards towards the body. The left foot draws into your right foot without the toes touching the ground, and moves out ahead of you to 9.00.

NOTES:

- In performance a little more can be made of the movement of the left sword-fingers; make a generous extension of the left arm, allowing the wrist to lead the movement to the left, and the fingertips to follow last of all (i.e. your fingers will point slightly to your right).

127

18.2

Alt. view

128

BRIEF:
Both hands into your waist.

DETAILS:
As you star to move the weight onto your left foot, *both* hands draw into either side of your waist, turning the palm (holding the sword) up, and bringing the left sword-fingers (palm up) to the left side of your waist.

NOTES:

- Keep the tip of the sword pointing in the direction of the thrust that is about to take place; beginners tend to let it drop at this stage.

- Keep the body upright.

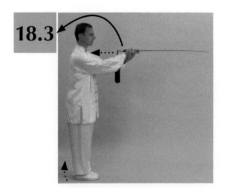

18.3

BRIEF:
Thrust.

DETAILS:
As you move the weight on to your left foot, thrust the sword directly ahead of you to 9.00, with the left hand sword-fingers now moving underneath your right hand (palm up). The left face of the blade is still upwards. As you thrust the blade forward with both arms outstretched, bring the right foot into the left, so that the feet are together, and straighten the legs.

NOTES:

- The knees are not bent at all in this posture.

- As before in Posture 14, instead of sword-fingers, the left hand can also be an 'open' hand in this posture (i.e. palm up and fingers together under the right hand). If this method is used, the hand is opened when it is moving upwards from the waist, before the thrust.

- Thrust the sword from the waist; this is different to Posture 13.

- The arrival of the sword must be synchronized with the arrival of the feet together.

PRIMARY APPLICATION NOTES:
Potentially a follow-up to the previous Posture. Having drawn your sword back over an opponent's sword arm, you then step into him and thrust.

	Dusting Into the Wind Left *(Lit. Dusting Into the Wind)*	Parry in Left Bow Stance *(Lit. Left Bow Stance – Lán)*
19	yíngfēng dǎnchén	zuǒgōng bùlán
	迎风掸尘	左弓步拦

APPLICATION:

拦 = **lán** (*pron. "lan" as in 'man'*) block; stop; break off midway; hinder; obstruct.

A perpendicular sword with the tip pointing diagonally downwards, and the action of the blade facing forward and up in a lifting action. In the final posture, the hand holding the sword should be at eye height, and the tip of the sword should be approximately at waist height.

The power point is in the middle and rear part of the blade. It is the deflection of an opponent's thrust by sliding his sword to the side, away from your body. Using **lán**, the sword acts like a shield to protect you, or to block an attack; it is a 'lifting block', and appears very similar to **liāo**, but this is a blocking not a cutting technique. In **liāo** the tip of the sword points away from you, but in **lán**, the blade is angled at 45° to your body. It also differs from **liāo** in that the blade is diagonal to the direction of your opponent; in **liāo**, the tip will point at your opponent.

Postures 19, 20, and 21 all use **lán**.

130

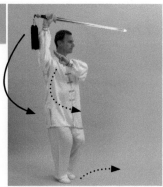

19.1

BRIEF:
Turn right toes, and rotate the sword.

DETAILS:
Start to turn your body to the right, turning the right toes outward 45° to 10.30 (pivoting on the heel), and putting the weight on to the right foot. As the weight moves across, turn and lift the left heel.

Simultaneously, rotate the blade anti-clockwise (your right palm turning to face away from you), allowing the pommel of the sword to pass underneath the right wrist. As the sword turns, lift the hilt up, so the pommel rises to eye height or above; the lower edge is now uppermost, the tip of the blade angled slightly downward, and the blade on a diagonal of 8.00/2.00.

The left sword-fingers touch the right wrist and follow the movement of the right hand.

The eyes look in the direction of the right arm, but avoid looking upward.

BRIEF:
Sink into the right foot; step to 7.30/8.00; circle the sword downward.

DETAILS:
As you continue to sink into your right foot, step diagonally to 7.30/8.00 with the left heel (i.e. with the toes at 45°), and start to drop the *hilt* of the sword (the tip now lifting) and circle it downwards in a clockwise vertical circle, so that the hilt is now below the tip. Circle the hilt downwards with the blade pointing to 1.30, and angled upward and pointing away from you at 45°. Allow the right elbow to lower towards the side of the body.

The left sword-fingers start to lower with the right wrist, but then separate to move palm up to the left side of the waist.

The eyes follow the tip of the blade.

NOTES:

- The wrist stays 'fixed' throughout this movement with the sword at approximately 90° to the forearm.

- Keep the right elbow joint open, and simply lower the right elbow, which will close into the body slightly.

- The hilt leads the movement with the tip of the sword following last.

- Keep the sword close to the body.

19.3

Alt. view

BRIEF:
Weight forward; **lán** (1).

DETAILS:
Transfer your weight on to your left foot into a diagonal left Bow stance, and simultaneously lift the blade *upward* and *away* from you, the hilt rising to the height of your face.

The left sword-fingers move from your waist, out to your left side, to rise above your head.

At the end of the posture, the body faces 7.30/8.00 and the blade is approximately on a 4.30/10.30 axis with the tip slightly lower than the hilt.

The eyes look to 9.00 (above the centre of the blade).

NOTES:

- As the sword lifts up, there should be a feeling of 'upward and away' with the blade; the 'upward' is self-explanatory, the 'away' requires an extension of the right elbow joint. It is *not* just a lifting up of the blade.

- This is a widened diagonal Bow stance; there should be 12 inches (30 centimetres) between the feet.

- As you raise the sword, parrying upwards, raise the hilt up the centreline of your body. Avoid closing up the right armpit by pulling the hilt to your left side.

133

- When raising the blade, part of the blade between the centre and the tip should be between your body and 9.00, i.e. make sure that it is a parry in front of you to 9.00. (This applies to Postures 20 and 21 also.)

PRIMARY APPLICATION NOTES:

This can be a block upwards with the centre of the lower edge of the blade. Your opponent is at 9.00.

This move can also be thought of as an attack to the underside of your opponent's wrist, after you have side-stepped his attack.

20 Dusting Into the Wind Right The Wind Flicks the Dust (*Lit. Dusting Into the Wind*)

yíngfēng dǎnchén

迎风掸尘

Parry in Right Bow Stance (*Lit. Right Bow Stance – Lán*)

yòu gōngbù lán

右弓步拦

APPLICATION:

拦 = **lán** (*pron. "lan" as in 'man'*) block; stop; break off midway; hinder; obstruct. (See Posture 19.)

20.1

BRIEF:
Sit back; circle the sword.

DETAILS:
Sit back on to the right foot, raising your left toes; turn the body and toes slightly to your left. As you do so, lift the hilt of the sword slightly, and start to arc it to your left.

The eyes look to 9.00.

20.2

Alt.
view

BRIEF:
Weight forward; right foot in; circle the sword.

DETAILS:
Move your weight forward on to your left foot with the toes pointing to 7.30, and bring your right foot into the left foot (without the right toes touching the ground). As you do so, continue to arc the hilt of the sword downward to arrive close to the left side of your waist, until the blade is pointing upward at approximately 45°.

The left sword-fingers meet the right wrist as your weight transfers on to the left foot, and remain there throughout the remainder of the movement.

The eyes look beyond the tip of the sword.

20.3

Alt.
view

BRIEF:
Step to 10.30.

DETAILS:
Step out to 10.00/10.30 with the right heel into a diagonal right Bow stance, (i.e. with the toes at 45° – pointing at 10.00/10.30). As you place the heel, the hilt of the sword moves further downward (close to your left thigh), so that the blade is virtually parallel to the ground.

The left sword-fingers follow the right wrist.

The eyes look to where the sword is still pointing.

137

20.4

Alt. view

BRIEF:
Weight forward; **lán** (for the second time in a row).

DETAILS:
Transfer your weight on to your right foot. The hilt of the sword arcs upward from your left side blocking up ahead of you again to face height.

The left sword-fingers follow the right wrist.

The eyes look to 9.00 (above the centre of the blade).

At the end of the posture, the body faces 10.00/10.30, and the blade is approximately on a 1.30/7.30 axis, with the tip slightly lowered.

NOTES:
(As above, Posture 19.)

PRIMARY APPLICATION NOTES:
(As above, Posture 19.)

21 Dusting Into the Wind Left The Wind Flicks the Dust (Lit. Dusting Into the Wind)

yíngfēng dǎnchén

迎风掸尘

Parry in Left Bow Stance (Lit. Left Bow Stance – Lán)

zuǒ gōngbù lán

右弓步拦

APPLICATION:

拦 = **lán** (*pron. "lan" as in 'man'*) block; stop; break off midway; hinder; obstruct. (See Posture 19.)

21.1

BRIEF:
Sit back; circle the sword.

DETAILS:
Sit back on to the left foot, raising your right toes. As you do so, circle the pommel of the sword further to your right whilst lifting it upwards slightly, and turn the body and toes slightly to your right.

The left sword-fingers remain on the right wrist.

The eyes look to 9.00.

139

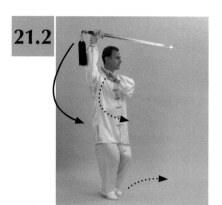

21.2

BRIEF:
Weight forward; left foot in; circle the sword.

DETAILS:
Move your weight forward on to your right foot with the toes pointing to 10.30, and bring your left foot into the right foot (without the left toes touching the ground). As you do so, continue to arc the hilt of the sword downward to arrive close to the right side of your waist, until the blade is pointing upward at approximately 45°. Allow the right elbow to begin to lower towards the side of the body.

The left sword-fingers start to lower with the right wrist, but then separate to move palm up to the left side of the waist.

The eyes look beyond the tip of the sword.

21.3

BRIEF:
Step to 7.30.

DETAILS:
Step out to 7.30/8.00 with the left heel into a diagonal left Bow stance (i.e. with the toes at 45° – pointing at 7.30/8.00). As you place the heel, the hilt of the sword moves further downward (close to your right thigh) in a verical clockwise circle. It can be 45° (as in the photograph) and parallel to the ground.

The left sword-fingers lower (palm up) and start to move out to your left side, prior to rising above your head.

21.4

Alt.
view

BRIEF:
Weight forward; **lán** (3).

DETAILS:
Transfer your weight on to your left foot. The hilt of the sword arcs upward from your right side blocking up ahead of you again to face height.

The left sword-fingers continue out to your left side, to rise above your head.

The eyes look to 9.00 (above the centre of the blade).

At the end of the posture, the body faces 7.30/8.00, and the blade is approximately on a 4.30/10.30 axis, with the tip slightly lowered.

NOTES:
(As above, Posture 19.)

PRIMARY APPLICATION NOTES:
(As above, Posture 19.)

141

22	**Pushing the Boat With the Current** *(Lit. Pushing the Boat Along the River)* shùnshuǐ tuīzhoū 顺水推舟	**Step Forward and Thrust Backward** *(Lit. Forward Step – Cì from Back)* jìnbù fǎncì 进步反刺

APPLICATION:

刺 = **cì** (*pron. "tsir"*) thrust; stab; prick; poke.

Thrusting the tip of the sword rapidly and powerfully straight at an opponent, the arm being extended from a bent position and making a straight line with the sword.

The power extends to the tip of the sword; if the blade-edges face left and right it is a flat thrust (*píng*cìjiàn); if the blade edges face up and down it is a perpendicular thrust (*lì*cìjiàn). The thrust can be directed upward, downward, forward, backward, sideways, or overhead in an inverted thrust. The power of the thrust comes from the back leg combined with the turn of the waist. Once you have committed to this movement, it can leave you open to a counter-attack, should you miss your target.

穿 = **chuān** (*pron. "choo-an"*) penetrate; bore through; thread.

A flat sword or vertical sword penetrating outwards in a different direction along the leg, arm, or body; the arm straightens out from a bent position; the power point is in the tip of the sword. The movement involves a turn of the body often of 180° or more, and can be seen as a method of converting a defensive move (to an attack from behind) into an attack (usually **cì**).

142

22.1

BRIEF:
Drop the tip as you step through.

DETAILS:
Turning your body to your right, transfer your weight fully over your left foot, and draw your right foot in alongside your left foot, keeping your right foot off the ground.

Drop the tip of the sword (with your right palm still facing you) so that the sword is 'dangling' almost vertically. To do this you need to relax the right wrist, allowing the little, ring, and middle fingers to open, and hold the sword loosely between thumb and index finger.

The left sword-fingers lower to touch the right wrist.

The hands are at face/throat height.

The eyes look toward the hands.

NOTES:

- You can literally allow the sword to 'hang', held only by the index finger and thumb. Don't try to hold it too tightly – the tip is in the process of thrusting through to 3.00 (in the 32-Posture Sword Form this is not an application as such), and the blade should be as close to your body as possible.

22.2

BRIEF:
Thrust the tip behind you.

DETAILS:
Step through to 9.00 with your right heel, turning it outward to 10.30 (it will turn further around as you transfer more weight on to it). The weight is still on your left foot.

Transfer more weight on to your right foot, turning it to point towards 11.00/12.00. Squat into a Sitting stance with your weight slightly more on the right foot, which is flat. As you do so, the hands separate and the left heel rises. The sword, with a perpendicular blade, thrusts to 3.00, the lower edge down.

The left sword-fingers separate from the right wrist, and extend to point to 9.00, with the palm facing *downwards*.

The eyes look towards the sword as it is raised, then to 9.00 prior to stepping.

NOTES:

- As the sword moves to 9.00, the tip passes very close to your right thigh. The body is very low, and initially, before the thrust, is angled forwards slightly.

Alt. height

- This movement is **chuān** 穿 = penetrate; bore through; thread. The feeling is of threading the tip of the sword from in front of you to behind you (in this case), keeping it very close to the waist, as if to hide it from an opponent who is behind you.

- This can also be done as a Half-Sitting stance – depending upon how low you wish to squat.

- When squatting, the lateral side of the left knee/lower thigh will press lightly against the lateral side of the right calf. Therefore, the thighs are close together; so it is important not to step too far ahead with the right foot in 22.1 above.

144

SECONDARY APPLICATION NOTES:

The tip of the sword 'threads' through to attack behind you. E.g. As your opponent thrusts at you, side-step with your right foot to avoid the thrust, partly turning your back to your opponent. Raise the hilt of your sword simultaneously, so that the tip drops (clockwise), and use the vertical blade to keep his sword away from you. Thread the tip through, pivoting on the feet, and thrust.

22.3

BRIEF:
Lift the tip, and place the left heel.

DETAILS:
Relaxing your right elbow, but keeping the right arm in the same position, raise the tip of the sword so that the blade is slightly past the vertical (the tip therefore angled slightly towards your head). Then step to 9.00 with your left heel. The left sword-hand still points (palm down) to 9.00.

The eyes look towards the blade.

NOTES:

- Avoid dropping the right wrist as you raise the tip of the sword.

- Bend your right elbow slightly and angle the blade towards your head – 30° (i.e. you need to level the blade off slightly for the thrust).

22.4

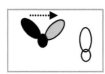

BRIEF:
Weight forward and inverted thrust.

DETAILS:
Turn your head to look to 9.00, and transfer your weight over your left foot as you thrust the tip of the sword to 9.00, with a perpendicular blade, the lower edge uppermost. The blade is angled slightly downward.

Your left sword-hand moves back and up to meet the right wrist.

The eyes look toward 9.00.

NOTES:

- When thrusting with an inverted sword, the movement should not be done with a straight right arm. In the previous Posture (2.3), when raising the tip of the sword, the elbow is very slightly bent; but on doing the thrust, bend it still further so that the power of the thrust comes, from the body, shoulder and elbow combined.

- In the final posture, your right wrist should be at the height of your forehead – no higher than the top of your head. Your right hand will be slightly to the right side of your head, but the tip of the sword will be between your body and 9.00.

- The tip of the sword should be at the height of your throat.

- Usually the application 'thrust' (**cì**) involves a line that is straight from the shoulder to the tip of the sword. However, in an inverted thrust, there will be a slight angle formed at the wrist.

- Relax your right shoulder. Keep the right elbow only slightly bent.

- Keep the body upright.

23

Flying Star Chases the Moon (Lit. Meteor Chases the Moon)	Turn Around and Chop (Lit. Reverse Body – Turn and Pī)
liúxīng gǎnyuè	fǎnshēn huípī
流星赶月	反身回劈

APPLICATION:

劈 = **pī** (*pron. "peee"*) chop; hack; split open.

A perpendicular sword coming forcefully downwards from above. The power is in the middle section of the blade-edge, and, at the moment of contact in the chop, both arm and sword form a straight line. **Lūn pī** means to describe a big circle and chop. The movement can be initiated from high up on either your left or your right side. The chop finishes either parallel to the ground, or with the blade angled downward at 45°.

23.1

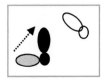

BRIEF:
Sit back and turn your left foot.

DETAILS:
Sit back on to the right foot turning the body to face 12.00, and pivoting the left toes inwards to face a minimum of 12.00. Draw the sword back (lower edge still up), so that the sword is between your body and 12.00 (with the tip still pointing to 9.00), at the height of your eyes, or just below.

The left sword-fingers still point at your right wrist.

The eyes look at the tip of the sword.

NOTES:

- The more that you are able to turn your left toes, the easier the step that follows.

23.2

BRIEF:

Sit back and separate the arms.

DETAILS:

Sit back on to your left foot and continue to turn your body to 1.30. Your left sword-fingers lower (palm up) to the height of your waist (left side), and the right hand, holding the sword, rises (as though holding the ball – see NOTES below), with the blade angled slightly downward behind you. Draw your right foot in beside the left ankle with the toes off the ground.

The eyes continue to look towards the tip of the sward.

NOTES:

- As you raise the right hand, there is also a feeling of circling the tip of the blade slightly.

- Note that the blade is angled slightly downward at the end of the move.

- When drawing in the right foot, avoid lifting it too high; the moving in of the foot is only a transitional move, prior to stepping, it is not a one-legged stance.

23.3

BRIEF:
Chop to 4.00.

DETAILS:
Place your right heel to 4.00, and then allow the sword tip to arc over your head, chopping to 4.00, to finish with the blade parallel to the ground.

The left sword-fingers circle from waist height, out to your left side and up over your head.

NOTES:

- In the final position, the blade and right arm should make a straight line.

- The angle of the right foot (facing 4.00) can cause a problem with the move that follows (which requires the left foot to move out to 12.00 – an angle of 120°). If you do not have good 'turn out', this can be extremely awkward for all level of students. It is probably easier (particularly for those with knee problems), to place the right toes so that they point at 3.00 or only slightly further than 3.00. This is not strictly correct, but ultimately less likely to damage the right knee in the move that follows!

24	**Celestial Horse Crosses the Sky** *(Lit. Heavenly Horse Goes Through the Sky)*	**Point Sword in Empty Stance** *(Lit. Empty Stance – Diǎn)*
	tiānmǎ xíngkōng	xūbù diǎnjiàn
	天马行空	虚步点剑

APPLICATION:

点 = **diǎn** (*pron. "dee-en"*) dot; point; poke; jab; strike at a vital point.

A perpendicular sword where the tip of the sword is used to prod downwards as if pecking; the power passes to the tip of the blade. Use the wrist to achieve this; the sword arm plays relatively little part in the stroke. The sword is mainly supported by the index and middle fingers; the other three fingers are relaxed. This connection of hand and sword therefore acts as a pivotal point so that the sword can move freely; it is important not to grip too tightly. This is not a large movement of the sword, but is usually quite a quick one. The purpose of **diǎn** is to attack an opponent's wrist, hand, or fingers of the arm that is holding the sword.

BRIEF:
Left sword-fingers and foot in.

DETAILS:
Without altering the direction of the sword, the left sword-fingers circle down to the right wrist, and simultaneously, the left foot draws into the right foot (with the toes not touching the ground) as the tip of the sword starts to drop slightly.

The eyes look at the tip of the sword.

24.2

BRIEF:
Drop (hang) the tip; left sword-fingers to the waist; left foot to 12.00.

DETAILS:
Without moving your right foot (which still points to 4.00), rotate your body towards 12.00. Simultaneously, rotate the lower edge of the blade clockwise, so that it is uppermost, and raise the hilt to head height, so that the sword is now approximately on a 12.00/6.00 axis, and the tip 'hangs' behind you with the blade pointing to 6.00.

NOTES:

- Avoid allowing the tip to hang too low; the blade should be angled no more than 45°.

At the same time, the left sword-fingers move (with palm up) down to your waist (on the left side), and your left heel steps out to 12.00, with the heel touching the ground.

Your eyes look to 12.00.

NOTES:

- All units of movement start and end together.

- This is a difficult movement mainly due to your right toes pointing to 4.00, which therefore involves a step with the left foot to an angle of 120°. The Kua needs to open as much as possible for the body to be stable.

152

BRIEF:

Swing the sword and sword-fingers over; drop the hilt.

DETAILS:

As you move your weight over your left foot, turn your toes out (to a maximum of 45°); your left sword-fingers move from the left side of your waist out to your left side.

The *hilt* of the sword starts to move toward 12.00 when half of your weight is on your left foot. The left sword-fingers circle to head height, and then start to move down towards the hilt of the sword, so that both hilt and left fingers lower together (although not at this point connected).

The hilt of the sword drops down in front of the centreline of your body (to approximately the height of your abdomen, and with the left sword-fingers connecting to touch the right wrist at the end of the drop). With the tip of the sword still upright, the right foot moves towards the left calf, without touching the floor (it is in the process of passing the left leg to move ahead into an Empty stance).

24.4

BRIEF:
Diăn as right toes step through.

DETAILS:
As you lift the hilt to shoulder height, push it away from you, and allow the tip to fall away from you to 12.00, to point at 45° downwards in **diăn**. As the tip arrives in the final posture, the right toes complete stepping through and touch the floor with the heel slightly raised, and with the ball of the foot and toes on the floor.

NOTES:

- As the sword drops down in front of you, prior to **diăn'**, keep both the right hand (holding the sword) and the left sword-fingers 'balanced', i.e. at the same height – they sweep down together in unison. As the right hand rises to 'point' sword, the left hand merely follows it.

153

Section 4

25	**Lift the Curtain** *(Lit. Hoisting Curtains on a Pole Posture)* tiáolián shì 挑帘势	**Stand on One Leg and Lift Sword Horizontally** *(Lit. One-Legged Stance – Flat Tuō)* dúlì píngtuō 独立平托

APPLICATION:

The following two strokes need to be mentioned together: They are virtually identical and teachers seem to differ in their explanations as to why they are called by different names. Some say that they differ only in the direction that the tip points, but others say that the function is slightly different for each – as explained below:

托 = **tuō** *(pron. "tour" as in 'more')* hold in the palm; support from underneath.

A perpendicular sword lifted upwards to past head height; the power is in the blade-edge (same as **jià** but the sword points to your right). This is a horizontal upward block, often with the thicker section of the blade nearer the hilt.

Some teachers say that **tuō** is one blade lifting another blade, i.e. the two blades are in contact and the lower one pushes up under and against the upper one.

架 = **jià** *(pron. "jee-ah")* put up; erect; support (as of a shelf); ward off.

A perpendicular sword lifted upwards to past head height; the power is in the blade-edge (same as **tuō** but the sword points to your left). This stroke follows the same principle as **lán** but the block is above the head. It is a horizontal upward block, often with the thicker section of the blade nearer the hilt.

Some teachers say that jià is a vertical lift of the blade, which, un-like **tuō** is *not* in contrast with the other blade, or limb, above it. So it is a forceful vertical lift into the opponent's weapon or limb.

25.1

BRIEF:
Anti-clockwise circle of the sword; step back.

DETAILS:
Turn your right palm up, allowing the tip of the sword to drop to your right towards 3.00. Turning the lower edge of the blade upwards, and starting to lift the tip, step diagonally backwards (back cross step) with the ball of the right foot to 7.30.

Keep lifting the tip, so that it rises vertically and then starts to drop on your right side pointing towards 9.00.

The left sword-fingers remain touching your right wrist.

The eyes follow the tip of the sword.

NOTES:

- Ensure that it is not the wrist alone which circles the sword; the centre should also be involved.

25.2

BRIEF:
Squat and press the blade.

DETAILS:
With the right toes cross-stepped behind you, squat or half-squat and press the blade downwards, so that the lower edge of the blade presses towards the ground with the tip slightly higher than the hilt. Allow the body to lean both forwards slightly and also towards the 10.30 corner. The hilt of the sword is between your body and 12.00, on the left side of your waist, with the blade out to your left side, and the tip pointing towards 8.00.

The left sword-fingers remain touching your right wrist.

The eyes look at the tip of the sword.

156

25.3

BRIEF:
Rotate the body; lift the blade and knee.

DETAILS:
As you begin to stand, rotate the body clockwise on the balls of both feet, gradually lifting the hilt of the sword. As you stand and turn your body (your centreline will face approximately 4.30), the blade rises as if spiralling upwards, the lower edge starting to turn upwards. The tip will be dropped slightly throughout this initial lifting of the blade.

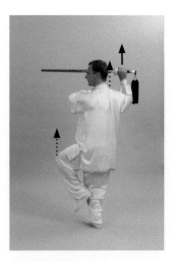

Keep rotating the body so that it faces 4.30; the blade has moved round between your body and 6.00, with the underside edge now upwards and at about shoulder height. The blade should now be parallel to the ground and pointing to 3.00.

At this stage, your left sword-fingers are still following the right wrist.

25.4

BRIEF
Raise sword and stand.

DETAILS
To complete the posture, lift the blade upward above your head, **tuō**, with the blade parallel to the ground, and the first third of the blade (nearest the hilt) between your head and 6.00. Lift the left knee high with the toes pointing down (the sole faces your thigh), and the knee pointing to 3.00. (See NOTES below.)

Your left sword-fingers should be at the right elbow or forearm.

Your eyes look to 3.00.

Alt.
view

NOTES:

- The pivoting of the feet: My personal preference is to pivot the right heel first on the ball of the foot, to place it flat, and then pivot the left heel on the ball of the foot. However, I have seen a 'double pivot' performed on several occasions, i.e. a simultaneous pivot on both feet. I personally think that this is incorrect as it raises the energy to the chest which makes standing on one leg harder.

- Avoid holding the blade too far away from you towards 6.00. This is a lifting of the blade to above the head.

- As in 2.3, and 8.2, the thigh being parallel to the ground is the *minimum* requirement.

PRIMARY APPLICATION NOTES:

This is a blocking upward posture to an attack from 6.00.

26

Wheel the Sword to the Left (*Lit. Left Chariot Wheel Stroke*)

zuŏ chēlúnjiàn

左车轮剑

Hook and Chop In Bow Stance (*Lit. Bow Stance – Guà and Pī*)

gōngbù guàpī

弓步挂劈

APPLICATION:

挂 = **guà** (*pron. "gwar"*) hang (something); suspend.

The sword tip is hooked backwards either upward or downward, from front to back, with a perpendicular blade, to keep the opponent away as he advances to attack, or to divert his attack. In effect, you hook your sword either downward or upward with the tip leading, so that the faces (sides) brush his weapon aside. The energy is therefore in the face of the body of the sword.

劈 = **pī** (*pron. "peee"*) chop; hack; split open.

A perpendicular sword coming forcefully downwards from above. The power is in the middle section of the blade-edge, and, at the moment of contact in the chop, both arm and sword form a straight line. **Lūn pī** means to describe a big circle and chop. The movement can be initiated from high up on either your left or your right side. The chop finishes either parallel to the ground, or with the blade angled downward at 45°.

159

26.1

BRIEF:
Step forward and hook the sword.

DETAILS:
This is a hooking action with the tip of the blade.

Bend your right knee, sinking the centre of gravity. Step forwards to 3.00, turning the left foot outwards to 45° (to 1.30), raising the right heel, and placing the weight on to the left foot. As you do so, without turning the blade, drop the tip, and arc it downwards in a generous hook to the left side of your body to point behind you. You need to keep the upper edge of the blade facing you throughout the hook, and the tip always leads the hook. This is a vertical circle.

Simultaneously, the left sword-fingers lower until they are palm *down* in front of your right shoulder or upper arm. The left wrist will be approximately above the right wrist.

The eyes watch the tip of the sword.

NOTES:

- Turn your body as far to 12.00 as you are able when hooking the sword.

PRIMARY APPLICATION NOTES:
Your opponent thrusts towards you. Hook your sword down, blocking, or sweeping his sword to the side, with the outside edge – this is **guà**. (This application of **guà** is then completed at 26.3 by using **pī** (chop) to the opponent.)

160

26.2

BRIEF:

Turn the hands and hold the ball; place the right foot.

DETAILS:

As you begin to raise the right hand and lower the left hand, turn the blade and the sword-fingers simultaneously; the blade rotates so that the underside edge is now upward (with the right palm now facing away from you), and the left sword-fingers turn palm up. Your eyes still look at the tip. The right foot moves toward the left ankle with the toes off the ground.

Continue to separate the hands into the holding ball gesture (i.e. palms face one another), allowing the tip of the sword to angle slightly downward behind you. As you do so, the right foot steps through, the right heel being placed at 3.00.

Your left sword-fingers should be palm up on the left side of your waist.

The eyes continue to look beyond the tip of the sword.

NOTE:

- The hand movements going into the 'holding ball' gesture are very similar to the end of the first section in Posture 6: 'Stand on one leg and cut with arm-swing', i.e. just before the move where you stand on one leg and cut downwards with the body angled slightly forwards.

26.3

BRIEF:
Chop to 3.00.

DETAILS:
Transfer your weight on to the right foot into a Bow stance, and chop downward to 3.00.

The left sword-fingers circle from waist height, out to your left, and up above your head.

PRIMARY APPLICATION NOTES:
(Continued from the PRIMARY APPLICATION NOTES for Posture 26.1) Circle the sword up and over and make a vertical cut (which is **pī** (chop)).

27

Wheel the Sword to the Right
(Lit. Right Chariot Wheel Stroke)

yòu chēlúnjiàn

右车轮剑

Circle Sword and Chop in Empty Stance
(Lit. Empty Stance – Whirl and Pī)

xūbù lūnpī

虚步抡劈

APPLICATION:

劈 = **pī** *(pron. "peee")* chop; hack; split open.
(See description for Posture 26.)

27.1

BRIEF:
Sit back, turn toes; then move forward and sweep the tip behind you.

DETAILS:
Sit back very briefly on to the left foot, and gently lift the tip of the sword. Then, turning the right foot out towards 4.30 (minimum), immediately move the weight back over it, lifting the left heel, and drop the edge of the sword down before sweeping the tip backward to 9.00.

Meanwhile, the left sword-fingers lower from their position above your head, down in front of your face, to heart height, with the palm down, and the fingers pointing towards the hilt of the sword.

The palm should be aligned with the centre of your body, in front of the sternum.

The eyes follow the direction of the sword.

163

NOTES:

- When sitting back at the start of the movement, sit back only enough to turn the right toes outward.

- In the final position, the body should face 6.00.

- Avoid leaning.

- When swinging the tip behind you, avoid touching the ground. Lead with the pommel of the sword, the tip following as though pulling on a rope; once you start to lift the hilt behind you (towards 9.00), allow the tip to sweep down and then rise to point to 9.00.

- This movement has the feeling of **liāo**. However, **liāo** is not part of Posture 27 in the 32-Posture Sword Form; there is no pause in the momentum here, and you should immediately rotate and chop to 3.00.

27.2

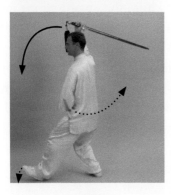

BRIEF:

Rotate the blade 360°; left sword-fingers to the waist; left foot through.

DETAILS:

As you rotate the hilt of the sword 360° in a clockwise direction (i.e. turn the sword over, without moving the tip – using the tip like a screwdriver), turn your body back to face 3.00, leaving your weight on your right foot.

Lower your left sword-fingers (with palm up) to the left side of your waist, and, bringing your left foot through past your right foot, place the heel ahead of you to 3.00.

As you turn back to 3.00, lift the hilt to slightly above your head.

NOTES:

- The sword is still pointing behind you to 9.00 with the lower edge of the blade uppermost, and with the tip slightly lower than the hilt as though it is 'hanging' behind you.

27.3

BRIEF:
Step through and chop downward.

DETAILS:
Continue the forward movement of the body towards 3.00, taking the weight on to the left foot (turning it out at 45°), and bringing the right foot through to finish in a right Empty stance.

Meanwhile, the sword chops to 3.00, with the tip angled downwards at 45°, and the tip at knee height.

Simultaneously the left sword-fingers sweep out to the left side, and arc upwards to approximately head height, and back down again to touch the right wrist, or forearm.

The eyes look in the direction of the tip of the sword.

NOTES:

- The movements of both arms are very similar to the arm movements in Posture 24 at the end of Section 3. However, the previous Posture is **diǎn**, whereas this is **pī**. Beginners often confuse the movements.

- In this final move, the moving arms 'balance' each other as they lower, the left sword-fingers mirroring the movements of the right hand.

- In the final posture, the back can be either upright, or angled forward *very slightly*; avoid leaning.

- Ensure that the right arm and sword form a straight line. This is not **diǎn**.

- There is often confusion between this Posture and Posture 24; there are certain similarities in moving into the final stance.

28	**Great Eagle Spreads its Wings** *(Lit. Great Roc Spreads its Wings)*	**Step Back to Strike Behind** *(Lit. Withdrawing Step – Reverse Jī)*
	dàpéng zhǎnchì	chèbù fǎnjī
	大鵬展翅	撤步反击

APPLICATION:

击 = **jī** *(pron. "jee")* hit; strike (e.g. a bell); throw (e.g. a stone); hammer (something); attack; bump into.

A flat sword flicked towards left or right; attacking towards the right is also called a flat **beng** stroke. The energy is released in a rapid movement by the forearm, and passes through the sword to the front edge of the tip. This can be an attack to an opponent's wrist, or throat.

Jī, **diǎn**, and **bēng** have similarities. **Jī** is to 'flick' with the tip – usually diagonally upwards and sideways, **diǎn** is to use the tip *down* as though 'prodding' or drawing a full stop with the tip, **bēng** is to use the tip *upward*. In the 42-Posture Sword Form the **jī** is done with power, but in the 32-Posture Sword Form it is done with a gentle, consistent movement.

167

Jiǎo is not one of the 13 applications, but should be mentioned as it appears at this point in the order of applications in the 32-Posture Sword Form.

绞 = **jiǎo** *(pron. "jee-ow" as in 'now')* twist; stir; mix.

A flat sword, letting the sword tip go clockwise or anti-clockwise as if describing a small vertical or horizontal circle in a twisting motion. The energy to the blade is produced, not by the wrist, but by the turn of the body.

28.1

BRIEF:
Circular movement with the tip (optional); turn right palm up, and step.

DETAILS:
Describe a small clockwise circle with the tip of the blade (see below – Option 1) and draw your right foot back alongside the left foot, with the right toes off the ground.

The left sword-fingers also describe a small clockwise circle (see below – Option 1) – working with the right hand, to finish with the left palm down, and either the left sword-fingers touching the inside of the right wrist, or the left wrist directly above the right wrist (palm up also).

The eyes look at the tip of the sword in both Options 1 and 2.

(See Option 2 below for a more straightforward method.)

NOTES:
Option 1:

- This action is done as though there is a fixed axis-point in the middle of the blade. In other words, were you to move the hilt 4 centimetres to the right, the tip of the sword would move 4 centimetres to the left, and so on:

- Lift the hilt slightly upwards and to your right (flexing your wrist); the tip will therefore travel slightly downwards and out to the left. As you do this, you are starting to turn the right face of the blade upwards.

- Continue by dropping the hilt (the tip will therefore rise), and finish by lifting the hilt back into the centre again with the face of the blade now up.

- The left sword-fingers can either stay fixed by the right wrist, or can describe a clockwise circle of their own simultaneously, to finish with the left wrist above, and almost touching, the right wrist.

- The eyes look at the tip of the sword.

- This action is performed as though the centre of the blade is a pivotal point. Gradually rotate the palm upwards, and as you do so, the tip of the sword describes a small clockwise circle – downwards, left, upwards, right. (This is a very subtle movement, and awkward to describe; the saying 'one showing is worth a thousand words' springs to mind. Having said that, beginners often experience some difficulty with this movement, even after seeing it!)

Option 2:

- Turn the right palm upwards, and move the left sword-fingers so that the left wrist is directly above the right wrist. As you do so, draw your right foot back alongside the left foot, with the right toes off the ground.

NOTES:

- Options 1 and 2: At the end of this part of the movement, the left face of the blade is upward.

169

28.2

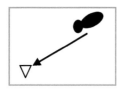

BRIEF:
Step back with the right foot; (optional arm movement).

DETAILS:
Step out with the *ball* of the right foot diagonally backwards towards 8.00 into a Side Bow stance. (Optional arm movement: You can also move the left sword-fingers further up the right arm (palm down), so that the left wrist is above the right elbow-crease; this is preferable as it closes the body up prior to opening it up in the following movement.) Otherwise, leave the left sword-fingers where they were.

NOTES:

- This is a Side Bow stance, so, whereas an ordinary Bow stance is greater in length than in width, a Side Bow stance is greater in width than in length.

- When stepping therefore, place the toes directly behind you to 9.00, but also slightly towards 6.00, thus slightly widening the stance when you eventually move into it. In the final posture, if you imagine a thick line of about 4 inches (10 centimetres) width, drawn from 3.00 to 9.00 between your feet, the heel of your right foot should be against one side of the line, and the toes of the left foot should be against the other side of the line. The right foot toes point to 6.00, and the left foot toes point to about 4.30/5.00.

28.3

Alt. view

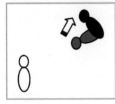

BRIEF:
Sweep the sword out to 7.00.

DETAILS:
As you move your weight on to your right foot, adjust your right heel so that the foot points at 6.00, and, with a loose wrist, sweep the sword towards 7.00 (the left face of the blade still uppermost); this is – in theory – a 'flick' of the sword (but it is performed *without* the 'flick'). As the weight moves over the right foot, slip the heel of your left foot.

The left sword-fingers are left behind in a straight line with the right arm, and the left wrist is flexed backward with the sword-fingers pointing sideways and therefore parallel to the ground.

The tip of the sword is level with the top of your head.

The eyes look to the tip of the sword.

171

NOTES:

- To execute the move correctly, the tip of the sword should arrive last. During its transition into the final posture, the elbow needs to gradually straighten – the shoulder and upper arm will line up first, followed by the upper arm and the forearm (i.e. the elbow straightens), followed by the forearm and the hand (i.e. the wrist will straighten last). If you imagine an object impaled on the tip of the sword, it may help to think of the action that you would make in trying to flick it off.

- In the final posture, the body is turned slightly over the right knee.

PRIMARY APPLICATION NOTES:
The **jī** stroke is a 'flick' to the neck or face with the tip of the sword.

29 Yellow Bee Enters the Cave (*Lit. Wasp Flies Into the Hole*)	Step Forward and Horizontal Thrust (*Lit. Forward step – Flat Thrust*)
huángfēng rùdòng	jìnbù píngcì
黄蜂入洞	进步平刺

APPLICATION:

刺 = **cì** (*pron. "tsir"*) thrust; stab; prick; poke.

Thrusting the tip of the sword rapidly and powerfully straight at an opponent, the arm being extended from a bent position and making a straight line with the sword.

The power extends to the tip of the sword; if the blade-edges face left and right it is a flat thrust (*píngcìjiàn*); if the blade-edges face up and down it is a perpendicular thrust (*lìcìjiàn*). The thrust can be directed upward, downward, forward, backward, sideways, or overhead in an inverted thrust. The power of the thrust comes from the back leg combined with the turn of the waist. Once you have committed to this movement, it can leave you open to a counter-attack, should you miss your target.

29.1

BRIEF:
Sit back, and cut to left and then right; sword parallel to the ground throughout.

172

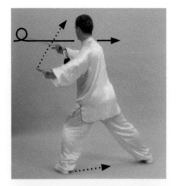

DETAILS:

Sit back on to the left foot, leading the hilt of the sword to your left at shoulder height (left face of blade uppermost, and blade parallel to the ground).

When the hilt reaches the 4.30 corner, reverse the sword, so that the tip now points to 3.00 (blade still parallel to the ground). Rotate the blade so that the right face is uppermost, and then, as the weight goes back on to the right foot again, lead the hilt to the right still at shoulder height (the lower edge of blade away from you throughout). The movement finishes with the blade parallel to the ground at shoulder height, the tip pointing towards 3.00. The centre of the blade is between your chest and 6.00.

As you move the weight back on to the right foot again (which has not moved and still points to 6.00), the left sword-fingers rise in a large arc, above your head, and down, to point at the right wrist in front of the right shoulder.

The left foot moves into the right foot with the toes at calf height.

The eyes look across the hands, i.e. towards 6.00.

Notes:

- As you cut to left and right, the tip of the sword will point to 9.00 as you cut left, and to 3.00 as you cut right. It is important to lead with the pommel.

- Use plenty of centre-turn for the cut to left and right.

- In the final posture, the left foot draws into the right calf, but should not be lifted too high as this is only a transitional move, and not a one-legged stance. This movement is sometimes done with the left knee turned out to point towards 9.00.

- The right foot does not move, but stays facing 6.00.

- The move has the feeling of **dài**, although this is not the application for this Posture.

SECONDARY APPLICATION NOTES:
Cutting across from left to right, or from right to left at throat height. Your left hand is possibly holding the wrist of your opponent's sword arm.

174

29.2

BRIEF:
Step, and both hands palms up by your waist.

DETAILS:
The body turns back to 3.00, and, as you place the left heel to 3.00, the sword moves down to the right side of your waist, with palm up. The blade of the sword is almost parallel to the ground, the tip very slightly lifted.

The left sword-fingers begin lowering to the left side of your abdomen, with palm up.

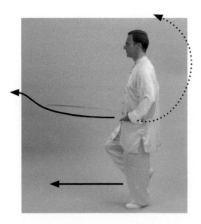

NOTES:

- This is similar to the move just before the thrust to 8.00 in Posture 10; 'Thrust in Left Bow Step'.

- The right palm, from being palm down in the previous movement (29.1), gradually turns to face your body as the sword lowers, and then finishes by the waist with palm up.

- Avoid pulling the elbows behind the body.

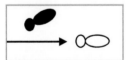

BRIEF:
Step and thrust.

DETAILS:
Turn the left toes out to 45° as you move the weight on to the left foot, and then step through with the right foot to 3.00, thrusting the tip of the sword also to 3.00 at chest height.

The left sword-fingers move from your waist, out to your left side, to rise above your head.

The eyes look beyond the tip of the sword.

NOTES:

- The width of the stance is between 4–8 inches (10–20 centimetres).

- Keep the body upright.

30	Embrace the Moon *(Lit. Hugging the Moon to One's Bosom)*	Withdraw Sword in T-Stance *(Lit. T-Stance, Turn – Chōu)*
	huáizhōng bàoyuè	dīngbù huíchōu
	怀中抱月	丁步回抽

APPLICATION:

抽 = **chōu** (*pron. "cho" as in 'go'*) lash; whip; draw out; extract; pull; take out; draw along; draw back (like pulling a draw out of a chest of drawers, or drawing a letter from an envelope).

A perpendicular sword drawn or whipped back towards the body, with either an upward or a downward *arc*. The point of power is either in (approximately) the centre of the blade-edge, in the length of the blade-edge, or in the centre of the ridge depending upon whether the stroke is used for attack or for defence. For example, the edge of the blade, if placed under a limb, would be pulled back to make a cut, whereas the centre of the ridge of the blade could also be used to block a thrust.

This stroke is often thought of as 'draw back' or 'pull back' like **dài**, and the principles of **dài** apply to **chōu**; but in **chōu**, the sword blade is perpendicular. This stroke is not just used to attack; it also adopts the idea of neutralization.

In this Form, **chōu** appears three times (Postures 7, 17, and 30), twice with an inverted perpendicular blade (Postures 7 and 30) in which the cutting or working edge of the sword is the upper one (an upward arc). In Posture 17, **chōu** occurs with the cutting or working edge of the blade being the lower one (a downward arc).

176

30.1

BRIEF:

Invert the sword and lift the blade.

DETAILS:

Turn the lower edge of the blade upwards and lift the hilt of the sword upward, leaving the tip of the sword in approximately the same position as in the previous move (i.e. do not raise it).

NOTES:

- This Posture is almost identical to Posture 7: 'Step Back and Withdraw Sword' at the end of Section 1.

- Stay in a right Bow stance.

30.2

Alt. view

BRIEF:

Sit back, arcing the hilt upward and then downward to your waist.

DETAILS:

As you sit back on to your left foot, arc the hilt upward, backward, and then downward to the left side of your waist (the tip will have risen by the time the sword has reached your waist). Draw your right foot completely into your left foot, with the toes of the right foot in a T-stance.

The lower edge of the blade is now upward at 45°. The distance of the hilt of the sword to your waist/hip is one fist's distance. Your right palm will be turned to face the body, the sword supported predominantly by the 'V' of the right thumb and index finger.

As you sit back, the left sword-fingers move down to touch your right wrist, on the left side of your abdomen.

In the final posture, the centreline faces 1.00/1.30; the right toes touch the ground in a T-stance. The sword is angled on a 10.00/4.00 axis, with the tip between your body and 3.00.

Your eyes look to 3.00 beyond the tip.

NOTES:

- This has been described as 'putting the pommel of the sword into your waistcoat pocket'.

PRIMARY APPLICATION NOTES:

The sword during this movement is making a cut, e.g. under an arm, or to opponent's hand or wrist. (E.g. If your opponent does **pī** (chop) to your head, you might side-step and lift the lower edge of your sword upwards under the hand with which he is holding his sword. You would then follow this with **cì** as in the following move.)

However, this can also be a defensive move, using the face of the blade to deflect a thrust.

31	The Wind Sweeps Away the Plum Blossoms (*Lit. Wind Sweep Plum Blossoms*) fēngsǎo meíhuā 风扫梅花	Turn Around and Wipe Horizontally (*Lit. Whirl Round – Flat Mǒ*) xuánzhuǎn píngmǒ 旋转平抹

APPLICATION:

抹 = **mǒ** (*pron. "more"*) wipe; smear.

A flat sword as if led across the neck from left to right or right to left; the power point follows the sword blade-edge in a smooth movement. This is a circling cut, and can be confused with **dài** or **sǎo**.

Alt. view

BRIEF:
Rotate the sword in front of your body, and take the first step.

DETAILS:
As you turn your centreline (now facing 1.30) to your right to face 3.00, start to turn your right palm so it begins to turn downward. Whilst doing this, allow the hilt of the sword to move with the body (with the hilt gradually rising to the height of the bottom of your breastbone/sternum). By now the right palm will almost be facing downward, and the tip of the sword will be moving to the left side of your body, and the hilt to the right side, changing the angle of the sword so that it is moving towards being parallel to the ground.

Immediately step with the right heel to 3.00, turning the foot so that it faces 5.30/6.00 (keep the weight on the left foot).

The left sword-fingers stay touching the right wrist.

The eyes look at the tip of the sword.

NOTES:

- At the end of this movement, the blade should be almost parallel to the ground, with the tip slightly raised, and the centre of the blade at upper chest height (although you sometimes see it higher).

- The initial turn of the sword and body can also be done leaning the body backwards, as though to avoid an opponent's strike. This creates more of a feeling of *circling* the sword in front of the body. When leaning, keep the sword parallel to the body, so that as the body leans backwards, the blade reflects the angle of the body.

180

31.2

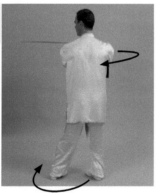

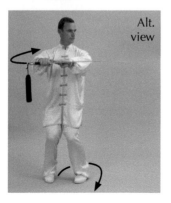

Alt. view

BRIEF:
The second step.

DETAILS:
Move the weight on to the right foot, and then place the left foot (stepping with the ball of the foot), so that the toes point at each other (pigeon-toed in a 'L' shape; a 'Turning-In' step – 扣步 kòubù) – this is like a 'hooking in' step.

The blade (still parallel to the ground with the tip slightly raised, and with the right face up), moves around with the clockwise turn of the body. The centre of the blade is held ahead of the centre of the body at chest height.

The left sword-fingers stay touching the right wrist.

The eyes follow the blade.

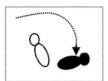

NOTES:

- The left foot should *step*, not sweep, around in an arc.

- It is the turn of the body that moves the sword; avoid attempting to move the arms independently.

- This rotation is often performed with the sword at throat height, although it is often also performed at the height of the upper chest.

PRIMARY APPLICATION NOTES:

This stroke can be an attack to an opponent's throat; it was originally taught to me as 'cutting off the heads'! It is 'smearing' from left to right with the edge of the blade.

31.3

BRIEF:
The third step.

DETAILS:
Step back to 6.00 with the right toes, and as the weight transfers on to the right foot, adjust the left foot by pivoting on the ball of the foot. As the weight finishes transferring to the right foot, 'balance' the arms by separating the hands to either side of your waist with both palms down, and held away from the body.

NOTES:

- The backward step is not directly behind the left heel, but is towards 5.00/5.30; this allows for the left toes adjustment at the end of the next move (see NOTES below).

31.4

BRIEF:
Move the left foot inward slightly.

DETAILS:
The left toes move into the centreline in an Empty step at the end of the move.

The tip of the sword is approximately in front of the centreline of your body, and the left sword-fingers point to 12.00.

The eyes look to 12.00.

NOTES:

- When stepping in all three moves, step with (1) heel, (2) toes – ball of foot, and (3) toes – ball of foot.

- It is not necessary to step directly back to 6.00 on the final (third) step; you can step as though to 5.00, i.e. into a slightly widened stance. The left toes will be adjusted sideways (to the right), and backwards slightly into an Empty stance to complete the movement.

- These three movements should be performed very smoothly with no break in the movement of the sword.

- Keep the body upright throughout.

- There is an alternative way of moving into Posture 31.4. It is possible for the left sword-fingers to stay with the right wrist until the sword has reached its final position (the body will have turned further to the right to face 1.30). Then, as the body turns back to face 12.00, the left hand separates and the left foot simultaneously moves into the centreline.

32 The Compass Points to the South
(Lit. Compass Needle Points South)

zhǐnánzhēn

指南针

Thrust Forward in Bow Stance
(Lit. Bow Stance – Straight Thrust)

gōngbù zhícì

弓步直刺

APPLICATION:

刺 = **cì** *(pron. "tsir")* thrust; stab; prick; poke.

Thrusting the tip of the sword rapidly and powerfully straight at an opponent, the arm being extended from a bent position and making a straight line with the sword.

The power extends to the tip of the sword; if the blade-edges face left and right it is a flat thrust (*píng***cì***jiàn*); if the blade-edges face up and down it is a perpendicular thrust (*lì***cì***jiàn*). The thrust can be directed upward, downward, forward, backward, sideways, or overhead in an inverted thrust. The power of the thrust comes from the back leg combined with the turn of the waist. Once you have committed to this movement, it can leave you open to a counter-attack, should you miss your target.

32.1

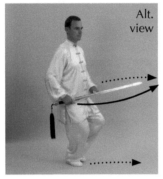

Alt.
view

BRIEF:
Both hands to the sides of your waist, and draw the foot in.

DETAILS:
Draw in your left foot beside your right foot (without the toes touching the ground), and bring the sword (with the lower edge of the blade downward, i.e. a perpendicular blade) and the left sword-fingers to either side of your hips.

The tip of the sword points to 12.00.

The left sword-fingers turn either palm downward or palm facing the body with the fingers pointing ahead of you.

NOTES:

- An alternative that I have come across is for the left sword-fingers, instead of moving inward to the left side of your waist, to move across your front toward your right wrist, reaching it only as you step forward into the following move.

- Some practitioners turn the body slightly to the right as the hands draw to the waist, almost like winding up.

32.2

Alt.
view

B<small>RIEF</small>:
Re-step and thrust.

D<small>ETAILS</small>:
Re-step to 12.00 with the left foot into a Bow stance, and thrust the tip of the sword to 12.00 with the lower edge of the blade downward (i.e. a perpendicular blade).

The left sword-fingers follow the right wrist, palm down.

The eyes look to 12.00.

N<small>OTES</small>:

- This is a widened Bow stance, 12 inches (30 centimetres) wide.

- Be careful to keep the left knee over the left toes.

- This is the only perpendicular straight thrust in the Form.

185

Closing The Form

C	**Closing Form** *(Lit. Closing Posture)* shōu shì 收势	**Closing Form** *(Lit. Closing Posture)* shōu shì 收势

APPLICATION:

The is the closing movement of the Form, and as such is really the return of the sword to the left hand. However, it could be seen as the flat of the blade blocking a thrust from 12.00 to your left.

C.1

BRIEF:

Sit back, turning to your right, draw the hilt back, palm on hilt.

DETAILS:

As you sit back on to your right foot again, turn your body to the right side. Bend your right elbow, and draw the hilt of the sword back between the top of your sternum/breastbone and 2.00/3.00. The blade remains parallel to the ground, with the lower edge still downward (i.e. your right palm will face your body). Leave the left foot flat.

The left sword-fingers follow the right wrist, but as the sword reaches its new position, open the sword-fingers into an open palm, in preparation for grasping the hilt of the sword, and place the palm of the hand on the guard with the fingers pointing toward the pommel and the thumb down. Your left elbow will be touching the left flat of the blade.

Turn your head to the right, eyes following the hilt.

NOTES:

- Make sure that you turn the body to your right.

- When sitting back, do not move or lift the left toes.

- Keep the hands level with the shoulders, and the elbows lifted so that the armpits are 'open'.

 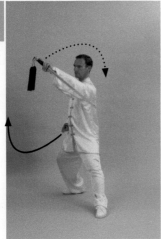

BRIEF:
Your left hand takes the hilt; hands start to circle as you move your weight forward.

DETAILS:
Take hold of the hilt and guard, with the left thumb close to the underside of the curve of the guard, the remaining three fingers curling over the top of the guard, and the length of the index finger in contact with the hilt. The heel of your left hand will be on the flat of the guard itself.

As you transfer the weight on to your left foot, take hold of the sword completely with the left hand and raise the hilt to the height of the top of your head, and towards 12.00. Start to lift the right heel.

The right hand forms the sword-fingers as it relinquishes the hilt and drops downward to waist height, before starting to circle upward, slightly behind you.

C.3

BRIEF:
Start to lower the hilt; right sword-fingers high; right foot in; knees still bent.

DETAILS:
As the hilt starts to lower to 12.00 and to your left side, raise your right sword-fingers into the air with a well-extended arm, and draw your right foot parallel to the left foot, a shoulders' width apart; both knees are still bent.

NOTES:

• Movements C.2 and C.3 are sometimes done without lifting the sword and hand above the head. The sword is pushed straight ahead to 12.00 with only a very slight lifting of the hilt. The right hand (now in sword-fingers) follows a similar path, with the elbow slightly bent, and the arm moving out side ways and forwards to 12.00, rather than rising above the head.

C.4

BRIEF:
Stand, lowering the right hand.

DETAILS:
As you lower your right sword-fingers to your right side, straighten your knees.

The left hand, now holding the sword, will arrive in position before the right sword-fingers.

NOTES:

- Movements 2, 3, and 4 are difficult to coordinate.

- Avoid collapsing the left knee in as you bring the right leg forward. Bring the front foot to alongside the left foot, and then move it sideways into a shoulder-width stance.

- When lifting the right arm, do not pull the arm behind the body; use the body's turn-back to 12.00 to help lift the arm.

- When lifting and circling the right arm upward, be careful not to lift the shoulder.

- In the final posture, keep the armpits open, and the left palm facing behind you.

C.5

BRIEF:
Feet together.

DETAILS:
Transfer your weight on to your right foot, allowing the crown of your head to rise, and your right foot to sink and, pushing your left toes into the ground, bring your left foot into your right foot.

NOTES:

- Relax both arms.

- Avoid bending the knees in order to bring in the left foot.

189

CHAPTER 4

Summary

CHAPTER

Footprint Map of the Form

I shall repeat the key to the footprint diagrams from p.47 for convinience

Left Foot   = | ●◗ | Black and dotted line e.g. ················▶

Right Foot   = | ○◗ | White and solid line   e.g. ──────▶

The arrow, depending upon its positioning, refers either to the direction of the next step, or to where the foot has come from.

The triangle ▽ or ▲ signifies toes down or toes up, and the colour again refers to right (white) or left (black).

'Slipping the heel' is shown by a thicker arrow which starts from the heel. It is a black arrow for the left foot (⬆) and a white for the right foot (⇧).

'Turning the toes' is shown by a short arrow: Either ····▶ (left) or ──▶ (right).

The diagram below shows how the clock directions (see p.48) correspond with the foot print map.

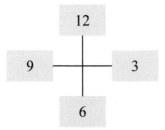

Opening the Form

Prepare

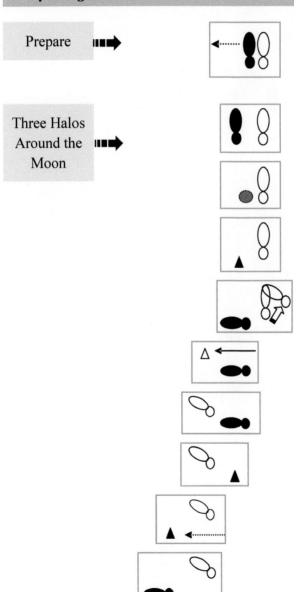

Three Halos Around the Moon

Section 1

Posture 1

Posture 2

Optional turn of the left toes

Posture 3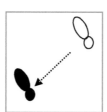

One-legged stance on the right foot

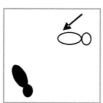

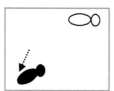

Posture 4

 Transitional
step with the
right foot

 Slight left heel
adjustment as
necessary

Posture 5

 Slight right heel
adjustment as
necessary

Posture 6

Left foot forward into
a one-legged stance
(off the ground)

Posture 7

Left Empty step – right
toes down

194

Posture 8

Section 2

Posture 9 ▮▮▯➡

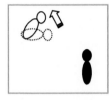

Slip the rear heel; this is a *Side* Bow stance

Left Empty step – right toes down

Posture 10 ▮▮▯➡

Slip your left heel

Slip your right heel

Posture 11 ■■➡

Weight on the right foot as you turn the left toes

196

Posture 12 ■■➡

Posture 13 ⊪➡

Posture 14 ⊪➡

This right heel placement is transitional

The left toes touch the ground

The right foot by left calf

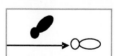

Posture 15 ▮▮▮➡

Right toes
briefly back

Posture 16 ▮▮▮➡

Left toes come back briefly
before re-stepping, but do not
touch the ground

Section 3

Posture 17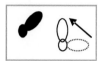

Optional turn back
of the left toes

Posture 18

Posture 19 ▮▮➡

Posture 20 ▮▮➡

Transitional sitting back

Posture 21 ▮▮▶   Transitional sitting back

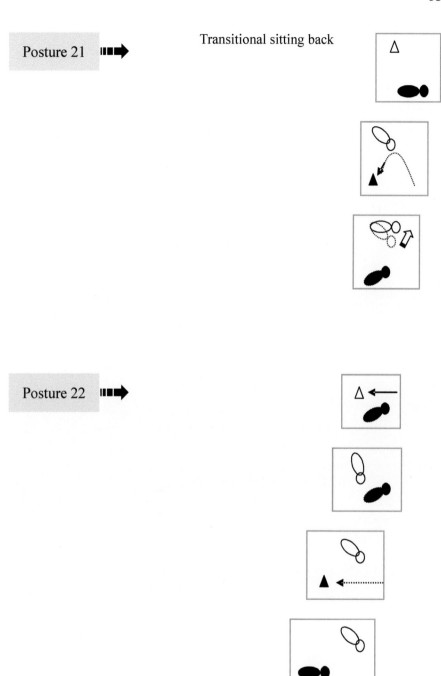

Posture 22 ▮▮▶

Posture 23

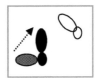

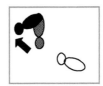

Posture 24 Left foot briefly into
the right ankle before
stepping to 12.00

Section 4

Posture 25

180° pivot

Posture 26

Posture 27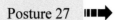

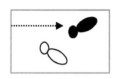

Posture 28

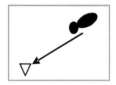

Side Bow
stance

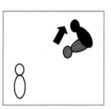

Posture 29

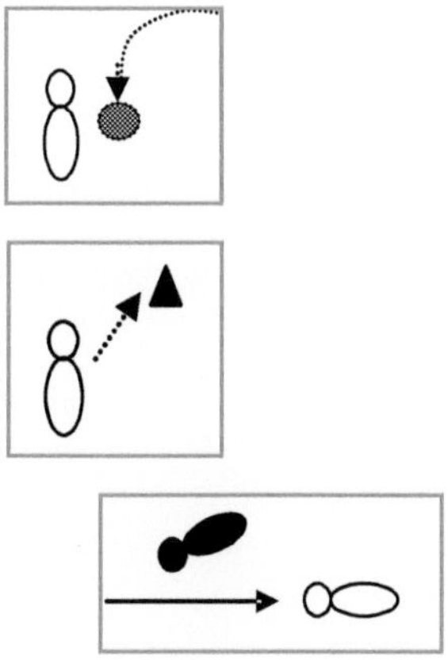

Posture 30 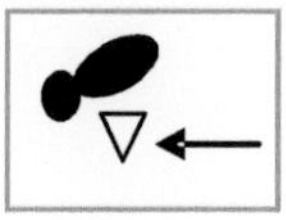   T-step

Posture 31

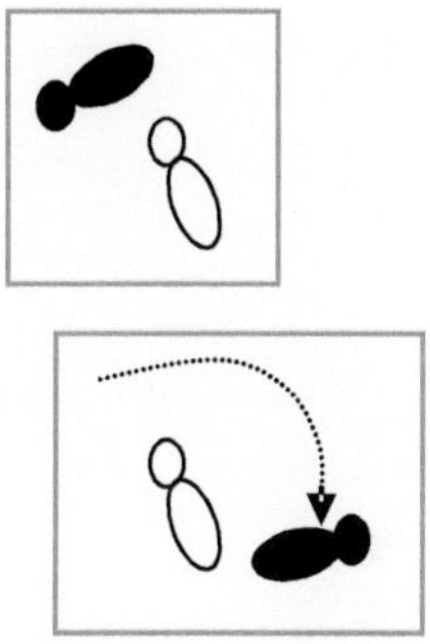

Left foot pivots
on the ball of foot

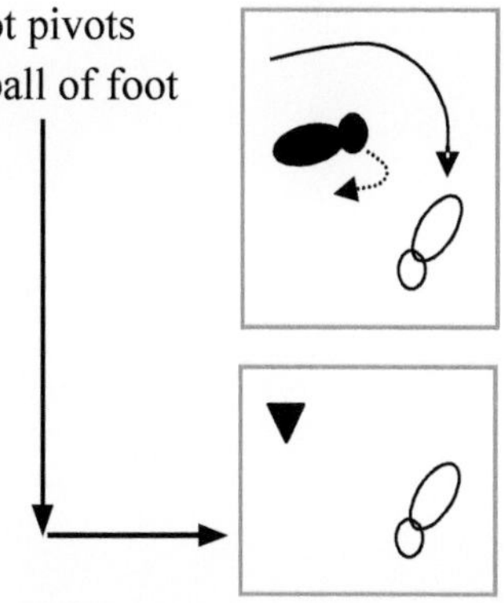

Move left toes
sideways

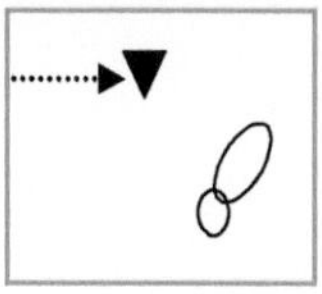

Posture 32

Closing form

Summary of the Form*

Opening the Form

Form	Traditional	Modern	Summary of movements	Repeats of Applications
		Initial Stance	Feet together, sword in left hand by side	
	Three Halos Around the Moon (san1 huan2 tao4 yue4) (sān huán tào yuè) 三环套月	Commence Starting Posture (qi3 shi4) (qǐ shì) 起势	1. Move left foot and stand with feet apart 2. Raise both arms to the front 3. Turn the body, swing the arms 4. Bow stance, point forwards 5. Sit and twist, extend the arms 6. Bow stance, grasp sword	

Section 1

Form	Traditional	Modern	Summary of movements	Repeats of Applications
1	**Dragonfly Alights on the Water** (qing1 ting2 dian3 shui3) (qīngtíng diǎnshuǐ) 蜻蜓点水	**Point Sword with Feet Together** (bing4 bu4 dian3 jian4) (bìngbù diǎnjiàn) 并步点剑	1. Drop hilt and **diǎn** stroke.	1 24
2	**Big Dipper** (da4 kui2 xing1 shi4) (dàkuíxīng shì) 大魁星势	**Stand on One Leg and Thrust** (du2 li4 fan3 ci4) (dúlì fǎncì) 独立反刺	1. Withdrawing step, **chōu** stroke 2. Gather in feet, **tiǎo** [pole] stroke 3. Raise knee, thrust (**cì**) from back	2 8 10 14 18 22 29 33
3	**The Swallow Skims the Water** (yan4 zi5 chao1 shui3) (yànzi chāoshuǐ) 燕子抄水	**Sweep Sword in Crouch Step** (pu2 bu4 heng2 sao3) (púbù héngsǎo) 仆步横扫	1. Withdrawing step, **pī** [chop] stroke 2. Crouch stance, sideways sweep **sǎo**	3
4	**Right Block and Sweep** (you4 lan2 sao3) (yòu lánsǎo) 右拦扫	**Horizontal Draw to the Right** (xiang4 you4 ping2 dai4) (xiàngyòu píngdài) 向右平带	1. Gather in feet, gather in sword 2. Step forward, push out sword 3. Bow stance, right **dài**	4 5 11 12

Form	Traditional	Modern	Summary of movements	Repeats of Applications
5	**Left Block and Sweep** (zuo3 lan2 sao3) (zǔo lánsǎo) 左拦扫	**Horizontal Draw to the Left** (xiang4 zuo3 ping2 dai4) (xiàngzǔo píngdai) 向左平带	1. Gather in feet, gather in sword 2. Step forward, send out sword 3. Bow stance, left **dài**	4 5 11 12
6	**Searching In the Sea** (tan4 hai3 shi4) (tànhǎi shì) 探海势	**Stand on One Leg and Cut with Arm Swing** (du2 li4 lun1 pi1) (dúlì lūnpī) 独立抡劈	1. Turn body, undercut [**lūn**; lit. whirl] stroke 2. Step forward, raise sword 3. One-legged stance, chop **pī** stroke	6 23 26 27
7	**Embrace the Moon** (huai2 zhong1 bao4 yue4) (huáizhōng bàoyuè) 怀中抱月	**Step Back and Withdraw Sword** (tui4 bu4 hui2 chou1) (tuìbù huíchōu) 退步回抽	1. Retreating step, raising sword 2. Empty stance, **chōu** stroke	7 17 30
8	**Evening Birds Returning to the Forest** (su4 niao3 tou2 lin2) (sùniǎo tóulín) 宿鸟投林	**Stand on One Leg and Thrust Upward** (du2 li4 shang4 ci4) (dúlì shàngcì) 独立上刺	1. Turn body, re-step 2. Raise knee, thrust **cì** stroke upward	2 8 10 14 18 22 29 32

Section 2

Form	Traditional	Modern	Summary of movements	Repeats of Applications
9	**Black Dragon Whipping its Tail** (wu1 long2 bai3 wei3) (wūlóng bǎiwěi) 乌龙摆尾	**Downward Intercept in Empty Stance** (xu1 bu4 xia4 jie2) (xūbù xiàjié) 虚步下截	1. Turn body, swinging sword 2. Turn upper body, downward **jie**	9
10	**Green Dragon Emerges from the Water** (qing1 long2 chu1 shui3) (qīnglóng chūshuǐ) 青龙出水	**Thrust in Left Bow Stance** (zuo3 gong1 bu4 ci4) (zuǒgōngbù cì) 左弓步刺	1. Step back, raising sword 2. Turn body, pull back sword 3. Gather in feet, gather in sword 4. Bow stance, flat thrust **ci** stroke	2 8 10 14 18 22 29 32
11	**The Wind Blowing on the Lotus Leaves** (feng1 juan3 he2 ye4) (fēngjuǎn héyè) 风卷荷叶	**Turn Around and Draw Slanting Sword** (zhuan3 shen1 xie2 dai4) (zhuǎnshēn xiédai) 转身斜带	1. Turn in foot, gather in sword 2. Raise foot, turn body 3. Bow stance, right **dài**	4 5 11 12
12	**The Lion Shakes its Head** (shi1 zi5 yao2 tou2) (shīzi yáotoú) 狮子摇头	**Retreat and Carry Slanting Sword** (suo1 shen1 xie2 dai4) (suōshēn xiédai) 缩身斜带	1. Raise foot, gather in sword 2. Withdrawing step, push out sword 3. T-stance, left dai	4 5 11 12

Form	Traditional	Modern	Summary of movements	Repeats of Applications
13	**Tiger Covers its Head** (hu3 bao4 tou2) (hǔbàotóu) 虎抱头	**Raise Knee and Hold Sword with Both Hands** (ti2 xi1 peng3 jian4) (tíxī pěngjiàn) 提膝捧剑	1. Empty stance, open arms 2. Raise knee, **pěng** stroke	13
14	**Wild Horse Jumps Over the Ravine** (ye3 ma3 tiao4 jian4) (yěmǎ tiàojiàn) 野马跳涧	**Jump Step and Flat Thrust** (tiao4 bu4 ping2 ci4) (tiàobù píngcì) 跳步平刺	1. Lower foot, gather in sword 2. **Pěng** stroke, thrust forward 3. Jump step, separate-hands stroke 4. Bow stance, flat thrust – **cì** stroke	2 8 10 14 18 22 29 32
15	**Little Dipper** (xiao3 kui2 xing1 shi4) (xiǎokuíxīng shì) 小魁星势	**Circle Sword in Left Empty Stance** (zuo3 xu1 bu4 liao1) (zuǒ xūbù liāo) 左虚步撩	1. Gather in feet, **jiǎo** stroke 2. Re-step, **jiǎo** stroke 3. Empty stance, left **liāo**	15 16
16	**Scooping the Moon from the Bottom of the Sea** (hai3 di3 lao1 yue4) (hǎidǐ lāoyuè) 海底捞月	**Circle Sword in Right Bow Stance** (you4 gong1 bu4 liao1) (yòu gōngbù liāo) 右弓步撩	1. Turn body, **jiǎo** stroke 2. Re-step, **jiǎo** stroke 3. Bow stance, right **liāo**	15 16

Section 3

Form	Traditional	Modern	Summary of movements	Repeats of Applications
17	**Shooting at the Wild Geese** (she4 yan4 shi4) (shèyàn shì) 射雁势	**Turn Around and Withdraw Sword** (zhuan3 shen1 hui2 chou1) (zhuǎnshēn huíchōu) 转身回抽	1. Turn body, gather in sword 2. Bow stance, **pī** stroke 3. Sit back, **chōu** stroke 4. Empty stance, point forward	7 17 30
18	**White Ape Offers Fruit** (bai2 yuan2 xian4 guo3) (báiyuán xiànguǒ) 白猿献果	**Thrust Flat Sword with Feet Together** (bing4 bu4 ping2 ci4) (bìngbù píngcì) 并步平刺	1. Re-step, turn body 2. Feet together, flat thrust – **cì** stroke	2 8 10 14 18 22 29 32
19	**Dusting Into the Wind Left** (ying2 feng1 dan3 chen2) (yíngfēng dǎnchén) 迎风掸尘	**Parry in Left Bow Stance** (zuo3 gong1 bu4 lan2) (zuǒ gōngbù lán) 左弓步拦	1. Turn body, **jiǎo** stroke 2. Step forward, **jiǎo** stroke 3. Bow stance, **lán** stroke	19 20 21
20	**Dusting Into the Wind Right** (ying2 feng1 dan3 chen2) (yíngfēng dǎnchén) 迎风掸尘	**Parry in Right Bow Stance** (you4 gong1 bu4 lan2) (yòu gōngbù lán) 右弓步拦	1. Turning-out step, **jiǎo** stroke 2. Gather in feet, **jiǎo** stroke 3. Bow stance, **lán** stroke	19 20 21

Form	Traditional	Modern	Summary of movements	Repeats of Applications
21	**Dusting Into the Wind Left** (ying2 feng1 dan3 chen2) (yíngfēng dǎnchén) 迎风掸尘	**Parry in Left Bow Stance** (zuo3 gong1 bu4 lan2) (zuǒ gōngbù lán) 左弓步拦	1. Turning-out step, **jiǎo** stroke 2. Gather in feet, **jiǎo** stroke 3. Bow stance, **lán** stroke	19 20 21
22	**Pushing the Boat With the Current** (shun4 shui3 tui1 zhou1) (shùnshuǐ tuīzhōu) 顺水推舟	**Step Forward and Thrust Backward** (jin4 bu4 fan3 ci4) (jìnbù fǎncì) 进步反刺	1. Step forward, gather in sword 2. Turn body, thrust backwards 3. Bow stance, thrust from back – **ci** stroke	2 8 10 14 18 22 29 32
23	**Flying Star Chases the Moon** (liu2 xing1 gan3 yue4) (liúxīng gǎnyuè) 流星赶月	**Turn Around and Chop** (fan3 shen1 hui2 pi1) (fǎnshēn huípī) 反身回劈	1. Turn body, gather in sword 2. Raise foot, raise sword 3. Bow stance, chop again – **pī** stroke	6 23 26 27
24	**Celestial Horse Crosses the Sky** (tian1 ma3 xing2 kong1) (tiānmǎ xíngkōng) 天马行空	**Point the Sword in Empty Stance** (xu1 bu4 dian3 jian4) (xūbù diǎnjiàn) 虚步点剑	1. Left hand to sword, left foot in 2. Turn body, raise sword 3. Empty stance, **diǎn** stroke	1 24

Section 4

Form	Traditional	Modern	Summary of movements	Repeats of Applications
25	**Lift the Curtain** (tiao2 lian2 shi4) (tiǎolián shì) 挑帘势	**Stand on One Leg and lift Sword Horizontally** (du2 li4 ping2 tuo1) (dúlì píngtuō) 独立平托	1. Interleaved step, **jiǎo** stroke 2. Raise knee, **tuō** stroke	25
26	**Wheel the Sword to the Left** (zuo3 che1 lun2 jian4) (zuǒ chēlúnjiàn) 左车轮剑	**Hook and Chop in Bow Stance** (gong1 bu4 gua4 pi1) (gōngbù guàpī) 弓步挂劈	1. Turn body, **guà** stroke 2. Bow stance, **pī** stroke	6 23 26 27
27	**Wheel the Sword to the Right** (you4 che1 lun2 jian4) (yòu chēlúnjiàn) 右车轮剑	**Circle Sword and Chop in Empty Stance** (xu1 bu4 lun1 pi1) (xūbù lūnpī) 虚步抡劈	1. Turn body, undercut (**lūn**) stroke 2. Step forward, raise sword 3. Empty stance, **pī** [chop] stroke	6 23 26 27
28	**Great Eagle Spreads its Wings** (da4 peng2 zhan3 chi4) (dàpéng zhǎnchì) 大鹏展翅	**Step Back to Strike Behind** (che4 bu4 fan3 ji1) (chèbù fǎnjī) 撤步反击	1. Raise foot, left hand to sword 2. Withdrawing step, **jī** stroke	28

Form	Traditional	Modern	Summary of movements	Repeats of Applications
29	**Yellow Bee Enters the Cave** (huang2 feng1 ru4 dong4) (huángfēng rùdòng) 黄蜂入洞	**Step Forward and Horizontal Thrust** (jin4 bu4 ping2 ci4) (jìnbù píngcì) 进步平刺	1. Raise foot, put sword sideways 2. Re-step, gather in sword 3. Bow stance, flat thrust – **cì** stroke	2 8 10 14 18 22 29 32
30	**Embrace the Moon** (huai2 zhong1 bao4 yue4) (huáizhōng bàoyuè) 怀中抱月	**Withdraw Sword in T-Stance** (ding1 bu4 hui2 chou1) (dīngbù huíchōu) 丁步回抽	1. Raise sword 2. T-stance, **chōu** stroke	7 17 30
31	**Wind Sweeps Away the Plum Blossoms** (feng1 sao3 mei2 hua1) (fēngsǎo méihuā) 风扫梅花	**Turn Around and Wipe Horizontally** (xuan2 zhuan3 ping2 mo3) (xuánzhuǎn píngmǒ) 旋转平抹	1. Swing feet, put sword sideways 2. Turn in foot, **mǒ** stroke 3. Empty stance, separate-hand stroke 4. Adjust left foot	31
32	**The Compass Points to the South** (zhi3 nan2 zhen1) (zhǐnánzhēn) 指南针	**Thrust Forward in Bow Stance** (gong1 bu4 zhi2 ci4) (gōngbù zhícì) 弓步直刺	1. Gather in foot, gather in sword 2. Bow stance, perpendicular thrust – **cì** stroke	2 8 10 14 18 22 29 32
	Closing Form (shou1 shi4) (shōu shì) 收势	**Closing Form** (shou1 shi4) (shōu shì) 收势	1. Sit back, grasp sword 2. Step forward for closing position 3. Feet together into original position	

CHAPTER 5

Beyond the Basics

The 32-Posture Sword Form in Competition

This is not a Competition Form, although it is often used as such. The following information about competition rules comes from the British Council of Chinese Martial Arts (www.bccma.com):

A warning will be given by the judges when a Forms competitor reaches the time limit (4 minutes) and if he does not finish the Form within 10 seconds, 1 point will be deducted from his score by each judge and he will be required to stop.

Sword, Spear, Stick, Sabre, Staff, Fan, and other weapons:
Points will be awarded, on a scale from one to ten, for the following criteria:

1. Correct posture.

2. Correct stance.

3. Distinguishing Yin and Yang.

4. Intent and focus.

5. Harmony of body and weapon.

6. Correct use of jìn.

7. Balance and agility.

8. Control of weapon.

9. Aesthetic appearance.

10. Martial spirit.

Music for the 32-Posture Sword Form

This Form can be performed to music, written by a student of Professor Li Deyin, who was also a music teacher in a High School in China.

In my opinion the music is too fast, and it is certainly too fast for use in competition, as the competition rules for the 32-Sword Form state that the routine should be performed in 3½ to 4 minutes, and the current recording, even with an introduction, is less than 3½ minutes.

There are two situations when it can be useful. The first is when performing in a very large group, which needs to be held precisely together, as at the Asian games when over a thousand people performed the 24-Posture Hand Form in the arena; music was specially composed for the occasion as the best if not the *only* way of holding the group together.

The second situation when music can be useful is when teaching Tàijí to beginner students in their first year, to encourage the flow from one posture to another. As most Tàijí teachers know, some beginners find it hard to move smoothly – to flow in the Form – and occasionally music can help.

Centre-Movement

Centre-Turn

The centre, Dantian, or core of your body plays a significant role in taijiquan. It initiates all movement in the body, including the bending of both elbows and knees, and the turning of the body from left to right. It is like the mainspring in an analogue clock – without the movement of the mainspring, none of the cogs will turn. For example, when you move an arm, it is the centre that moves first – perhaps by a nano-second, and it is important to feel the centre's involvement in creating the action of arm-movement. There is an expression in Chinese martial arts which states that: 'Energy is initiated in the foot, controlled by the waist, and manifested in the hand'. In reality this expression should read:

'Energy is initiated by the centre, reflected by the foot, controlled by the waist, and manifested in the hand'.

'Centre-Turn' refers (in this terminology) to the way in which you move the centre on a horizontal plane. In other words, this is the way that you turn your centre when moving from left to right, or forwards and backwards. E.g. when walking, your centre will turn towards the leg that you place in front of you; if it doesn't, and you turn it the other way, you will walk like Frankenstein! Therefore, when walking, if you place your left foot in front of you and move on to it, this would be called 'centre left' – you can call it left and forward, but it isn't strictly speaking quite true, because 'forward' is slightly different – there is no turn of the body. To exemplify:

1. If you do the first movement of the 32-Posture Sword Form (after stepping sideways with the left foot), by lifting up the hands (one holding the hilt of the sword) ahead of you, this move is '*centre back*'; if you didn't move the centre back at this stage and kept your body in exactly the same place in space as it was before you lifted the hands, the body would fall forward simply because there is the weight of both arms and the sword in front of you... basic body mechanics.

2. If you were now to lower the right hand and the hilt back to your sides again (e.g. as at the very end of the Form), this would be '*centre forward*'.

3. In the Form, there are many examples of the centre turning to left or right, but not so many of forward and backward. Other examples of centre back would be both final **diǎn** postures that are Postures 1 and 24.

4. Further examples of left and right would be Posture 4: From the final posture of Posture 3 (**sǎo**), the centre turns left as you draw the blade in, right as you push it out, and right again as you turn the blade and draw the sword to the right.

The point is that it is the centre, Dantian, or core that makes the move; the arms do not work independently – Tàijí is a whole-body exercise.

'Opening' and 'Closing'

There are certain places where the body 'opens' and 'closes'; this refers to the use of the Dantian or 'centre' on the vertical plane. An 'open' move becomes more obvious when you know how to 'close' the body.

The simplest description of the body closing is when you sit down on your heels in a squat; the centre of the body has compressed, or 'closed', and the 'Kua' (see above) folds. It is almost impossible to do this if you push out your abdomen, and in fact it's necessary to do completely the opposite – pull your abdomen *inwards*. So what you do is to *physically* pull your lower abdomen in – gently tighten the lower stomach muscles (it should feel as though you are pulling your navel upwards and also towards your spine), and compress the centre.

This has a number of effects on the body, but the most important is that it draws everything inwards, and in particular your elbows and knees. It is as though the body is a loading spring, ready to expand outwards again – a tiger/leopard/puma, etc. about to pounce. It is also the body protecting its centre/core, and can be seen in many animals and insects – a woodlouse, an armadillo, a pangolin, or a hedgehog, as they roll themselves up.

Pulling your lower abdomen inwards actually causes the front of the pelvis to tilt upwards, or lift, and it very important to simultaneously soften or release the area of the sacrum, which will therefore allow the rotation to take place. An analogy of this is to hold a football between your hands; if you roll the ball, e.g. you might lift your right hand, this means that, to keep the ball at the same place in space, you will need to lower your left hand. You cannot leave the left hand stationary, otherwise the ball will move to a different place. You need to achieve the same effect with the body – leaving the centre at the same point in space.

It is slightly more complicated than this in the Tàijí Form because there are moments when the Dantian closes and the chest might or might not close; it depends upon the movement and on what is trying to be achieved – often on whether you are trying to return qì to the Dantian or not.

A rather simplified version of how this is done in Tàijí is as follows: Stand on one foot and extend the other heel placing it on the floor ahead of you (toes raised), but as yet with no weight on it. This is in fact a slightly closed movement already, as the thigh has started to lift towards the abdomen. To fully close, as you place the front foot flat, pull the abdomen inwards (as discussed above), and allow the hip/pelvis to fold further the body will now be angled forwards slightly, and the back/spine will be slightly rounded. The weight might shift slightly on to the front foot, but it will be minimal, and it possibly won't need to (this depends upon the posture). During the above, the arms/elbows will almost definitely be moving in closer to the body, and there should be a feeling of the body 'compressing' into the centre. (See example 1 below.)

In reality, it is *not* the body 'compressing' into the centre, it is the reverse – it is the centre drawing the body into itself. I have in mind as an analogy the way that a squid or a jellyfish propels itself through the water – compress and release, compress and release, etc.

'Opening' therefore becomes obvious: Move out of the posture, and the centre undoes and 'opens'. Press the foot that you are moving on to into the ground, allowing the energy to rise. Examples of this are:

1. A 'closed' movement is in the opening section 'Three Halos Around the Moon'. As you step to the left with the left heel for the first time, the body is starting to close; as you put the foot flat the centre closes completely.

2. Another example of a 'closed' posture is Posture 1 (**diǎn**). The body is 'closed' – lower abdomen pulled in and tailbone tucked under. The chest is also 'closed'.

3. An example of a 'closed' position followed immediately by an 'open' posture would be Posture 28 (**jī**). As you step with the right foot into the Side Bow stance, the centre and chest 'close' like springs coiling and compressing. As you move into the final posture of jī, the chest and centre 'open'.

I have chosen the above examples, not because they are the only ones – there are a great many more, but because they are relatively clear. However, because there are various degrees of closed-ness, it is simply too complicated to describe which moves are 'slightly closed' (i.e. in the process of 'closing'), or 'fully closed', or where, for example, the chest and only the right Kua is closed, or the left arm and the right hip.

About the Author

James Drewe became involved in the Chinese Health Arts in 1975 when he began studying Gōngfu and Tàijíquán. He rapidly became interested in the philosophy behind these forms of exercise and also in both meditation and the use of diet to promote health. Since then he has taken an interest in a variety of other health arts and qualified as an acupuncturist.

In 1980 he began learning the Yang family style of Tàijíquán and Zhàn Zhuāng Qìgōng under Master Chu King Hung and has also studied Zhàn Zhuāng Qìgōng with Master Lam Kam Chuen.

He later broadened his Tàijí training with Richard Watson, learning the core syllabus of both Hand and Sword Forms of the 'modern' Yang style; he has also studied many of these with both Professor Li Deyin and Master Wang Yanji.

James has also studied the following forms: Chen 56-Step Competition Form, the Wudang Tàijí Sword Form, and the Chen Broadsword with Simon Watson; the Sun 97-Step Form, the Yang Broadsword, and the Fan Form with Professor Li Deyin; and the Sun 73-Step Competition Form with both Simon Watson and Master Huang Ping.

In Qìgōng, apart from Zhàn Zhuāng Qìgōng, he has studied a therapeutic Qìgōng called Dàoyin Yǎngshēng Gōng, which consists of sets of exercises for the cardiovascular, digestive, respiratory, and skeletal systems, as well as exercises for the 5 major organs with Richard Watson, Mark Atkinson, Hu Xiao Fe, and Professor Zhang Guande.

James is Vice-Chairman of the Longfei Tàijíquán Association, and runs classes in both London and Kent. He currently teaches a wide variety of forms, which are taught alongside pushing hands, dà lù, applications of the forms, and fā jìn techniques. Details of courses and classes can be found on www.taiji.co.uk, and www.qigonghealth.co.uk and James can be emailed at james@taiji.co.uk.

Further Reading

Chen, W.M., translated by Barbara Davis (2000) *Taiji Sword and other Writings*. Berkley: North Atlantic Books.

China Sports Editorial Board (1988) *Taiji: 48 Forms & Swordplay*. Beijing: Foreign Languages Press.

Deyin, L. and Dong, Z.H. (1997) *Sanshier-shi Taijijian: Jiao Yu Xue*. Beijing: Beijing Sports University Publications.

Dolbear, D.F. (2008) *An Introduction to Antique Chinese Swords of the Qing Dynasty Period*. Available at http://northernwu.com/swordgrp.htm

Tseng J.P. (1982) *Tai Chi Weapons (Weapons of Primordial Pugilism)*. London: Paul H. Crompton Ltd.

Yang, J.M. (1999) *Taiji Sword, Classical Yang Style*. Boston: YMAA Publication Center.

Zhang, Y. (1998) Manual of Taiji Jian. *The Art of Chinese Swordsmanship*. Boston: Weatherhill.